JUDO

Syd Hoare started Judo in 1954 at the age of fifteen. He joined the Budokwai – Britain's premier club – and within eighteen months won his Black belt against adult opposition. His promotion to Black belt at the age of sixteen was the youngest ever.

At seventeen he was captain of the London Area team that won the National Area Team Championships. In the same year, 1957, he was selected to represent Britain in the European championships. Military service intervened during which time he served in Cyprus and Germany. After military service he fought once more in the London Area team which again won the National Area Team championships. In 1961, at the age of 21, he set sail for Japan and trained there for nearly four years. On his return from Japan, with a grade of 4th Dan, he was selected to represent Britain in the Tokyo Olympics of 1964. He fought in the British team from 1964 to 1968 and in 1965 he won the silver medal in the Open weight category of the European championships.

He retired from active competition in 1968 and was appointed Chief Instructor of the Budokwai – a post he still holds. From 1968 to 1971 he read Japanese at London University and then did three years post-graduate research into Japanese Buddhism.

During his time as Chief Instructor at the Budokwai he has trained many young men up to Olympic medal standard, European gold medal standard and British championship level. In addition to competing and instructing, he has written several books on Judo, commentates for ITV and plays an active role in the administration of the British Judo Association.

D1188811

TEACH YOURSELF BOOKS

JUDO

Syd Hoare

TEACH YOURSELF BOOKS
Hodder and Stoughton

First printed 1980
Second impression 1982

Copyright © 1980
Syd Hoare

British Library C.I.P.

Hoare, Syd
    Teach yourself judo. – 2nd ed. – (Teach yourself
books).
    1. Judo
    I. Title   II. Series
    796.8′152   GV1114

    ISBN 0–340–24786–X

Printed and bound in Great Britain for
Hodder and Stoughton Educational,
a division of Hodder and Stoughton Ltd,
Mill Road, Dunton Green, Sevenoaks, Kent,
by Richard Clay (The Chaucer Press) Ltd, Bungay, Suffolk

Contents

List of illustrations

List of Illustrations

Foreword

If you went into different Judo clubs around the world you would find Judo done in different ways, and if you asked the club teacher about this he would say Judo has such and such a purpose and that is how I teach it. In fact Judo can be done for a variety of reasons and it is not possible to say that Judo has one purpose. A teacher may care to stress only one reason and that is perfectly valid but he cannot deny the other purposes of Judo.

Basically, there are five ways of looking at Judo. Jigoro Kano, the originator of Judo, said that judo is three things. It is a combat form, a physical training method and a character-building method. In recent years part of Judo has developed into an international competitive sport. In addition the vast majority of people who practise it in small clubs have discovered they like doing it for its own sake and can be said to do it for recreational purposes. Judo is also a Japanese activity. The 'style' or 'image' of Judo is Japanese and to many this is one of its attractive features.

In this book I have tried to cover all these aspects and stress the fact that Judo is an all purpose activity. For the modern competitive Judoman I have included chapters on modern training methods and contest tactics and for the more traditionally minded, chapters on Judo philosophy and Kata.

Judo has something for everybody. It is a completely natural activity for children, being a disciplined form of playground rough and tumble. It is a tough and demanding sport that will challenge any man (or woman) and its philosophical problems will satisfy the thinker who wants his sport to be more than just a sport.

Judo is rapidly developing as an Olympic sport. In the process the rules are being modified not only for competitive purposes but also to make it visually more exciting for the spectator. The result of this is to move Judo partially away from some of its original purposes. At a lower recreational level many of these developments do not apply. However, it seems to me that while Judo changes at the top of the pyramid, the base will probably want to carry on as it has done for nearly a century and that is why this book is fairly Japanese in flavour.

Although this book is in the Teach Yourself series it is anticipated that the vast majority of people who buy it will join a Judo club and learn their Judo as it were 'with the book in one hand'. Nevertheless the individual in some remote spot may learn a lot from it.

Since the majority of people who do Judo are male, I have described it from this point of view throughout, using the masculine gender. Women's competitive Judo is now flourishing and I hope that some of the 'fighting' ladies will not take this amiss.

Finally I hope the reader will get as much pleasure out of Judo as I do. I still learn something new almost every time I go on the mat and this is after nearly twenty-five years of training.

S.R.H.
Budokwai,
London, 1980

1
About Judo

History of Judo

Traditionally, Judo, or to give it its full name, Kodokan Judo, is the name
of a system of combat, physical training and character building devised
by Jigoro Kano and founded in 1882 in Tokyo, Japan. Judo means the
'Way of non-resistance'; it is often translated as the 'Gentle Art' but this
is not quite correct, since being thrown or strangled is rarely gentle. JU
means the opposite of 'GO' or 'hard, resistant', and implies that force is
never resisted but given way to and then used upon itself.

The techniques of Judo are derived largely from Ju-jitsu, which has an
ancient history. In times of peace or war the Samurai warriors of feudal
Japan were required to train daily in a variety of military exercises such
as horsemanship, swordsmanship and unarmed combat. The unarmed
combat was known as Ju-jitsu and various masters established their own
styles, methods and schools over the country. The earliest known school
is the Take-no-uchi-ryu, which was established in the mid-sixteenth
century.

A typical Ju-jitsu (sometimes written Ju-jutsu or Jiu-jiutsu) style might
contain a variety of moves such as kicking and punching, use of small
weapons such as a knife and defences against same, throws, joint-locks,
strangles and methods of tying people up. Mostly these were practised in
pre-arranged sequences, though a few schools practised free-fighting.

As a boy, Jigoro Kano had suffered at the hands of school bullies and in his resolve to do something about this he took up Ju-jitsu. Kano started by learning and mastering two styles of Ju-jitsu – the Tenjinshinyo and Kito styles which were quite widely practised in Japan. The Kito school of Ju-jitsu specialised in throwing techniques and the Tenjinshinyo school specialised in striking techniques and fighting on the ground.

Then he carried his studies further by talking to various surviving masters of other schools and collected their traditional documents. Ju-jitsu, like many other aspects of feudal Japan, had wilted under the impact of Western culture and was in danger of dying away and many of the surviving masters were keen to pass their knowledge on.

Eventually Kano put together his own system, calling it Judo to distinguish it from Ju-jitsu, and he called his school the Kodokan. Compared with Ju-jitsu, Judo placed much greater emphasis on throwing techniques, and included many new techniques devised by Kano. It had much better training methods with far profounder technical and moral principles. Kano said that Judo was not just a combat method as was Ju-jitsu but that it was a form of character and physical training.

At first Judo was like any other Ju-jitsu school but such was the calibre of its founder and the men who were attracted to his methods that it rapidly grew in size. During the early years the Ju-jitsu schools were jealous of this success and it is said that in the Kodokan one of the top men was always on hand to take on any challenges from visiting Ju-jitsu experts.

Finally the rivalry boiled up to a big public match in 1886 between the Kodokan and the representatives of various Ju-jitsu schools; the Kodokan won hands down. From then on the Kodokan went from strength to strength and the Ju-jitsu schools virtually disappeared.

Judo quickly gained a vast following in Japan and then began to develop overseas. Perhaps the earliest club to be founded outside Japan was the Budokwai in London which was founded in 1918. The height of Judo's international recognition was 1964, when it was included as a sport in the (Tokyo) Olympics for the first time. In these Olympics the Japanese dominated, as expected, but in the unlimited weight category class the Dutch Anton Geesink beat the Japanese Akio Kaminaga in the final, showing the rising strength of Judo in the West. A short while before this the Soviet Union had entered into world Judo and quickly gained a strong position.

Traditional Judo

Kano put together a neat yet comprehensive system. The full scope of Judo is not often understood by Judoka (practitioners of Judo) who tend to think of it as Sport Judo which is only one aspect of Judo.

Technically, traditional Judo consists of three main branches:

1. throws
2. groundwork (strangles, joint-locks, holds)
3. striking techniques (kicking and punching)

The throws are grouped together into what is known as the Gokyo or Five Teachings, which number forty throws in all. Groundwork, which means the techniques of fighting when both combatants have fallen to the ground, can be roughly divided into immobilisation techniques and submission techniques. The submission techniques, if carried to their extremes, can severely injure or kill the opponent. The striking techniques consist of all manner of ways of hitting an opponent with the hands, feet, elbows and so on. The areas that the blows are aimed at are known as the Kyusho or vital nerve spots of the opponent's body.

Traditional Judo is learned in two main and two subsidiary ways. They are:

1. free-fighting (Randori)
2. pre-arranged sequences (Kata)
3. lectures (Kogi)
4. discussion (Mondo).

Free-fighting is the main learning method of Judo. Here the Judomen actually fight each other but under a set of safety rules which exclude the more dangerous techniques. Sport Judo is in fact free-fighting Judo.

The pre-arranged sequences or Kata are for training in the basic principles and techniques and they are also the method by which the more dangerous are kept and practised in Judo. In the pre-arranged sequence the attack and defence moves are worked out in advance. The attacks are always done in the same way and the defences similarly. Both men practise the set moves countless times till each move is smooth, polished and automatic.

Judo now has seven Kata plus a more recently devised system of self-defence known as the Goshinjitsu.

The Kata are:

Nage no Kata	(throws)
Katame no Kata	(groundwork)
Kime no Kata	(self-defence)
Koshiki no Kata	(throws)
Itsutsu no Kata	(throws)
Ju no Kata	(throws)
Seiryoku-Zenyo	(punches and kicks)
Kokumin Tai-iku no Kata	

For a more detailed explanation of the Kata, see Chapter 13.

The two main technical and mental principles are:

1. Best Use of Mind and Body (Seiryoku-zenyo) and
2. Mutual welfare and benefit (Jitakyoei)

The first can be paraphrased 'maximum efficiency, minimum effort', and the second means that one best helps oneself by helping others.

On a more specifically technical level the main principles are: JU, or using the opponent's force against himself (more for defensive moves); Kuzushi, or getting the opponent off balance (more for offensive moves); and Shizentai which means 'natural posture' and is the basic stance of Judo.

Kodokan Judo has a number of traditional functions and they are:

The Five Article Oath (Gokajo no seimon)	This is the oath sworn by new-comers to Judo
The Opening of the Dojo Ceremony (Kagami biraki-shiki)	Held at New Year. It is a ceremony celebrating all aspects of Judo.
Monthly Promotional Contests (Tsukinami shiai)	Contests in which Judoka fight for higher grades.
The Red and White Spring and Autumn Contests (Kohaku-shiai)	Judoka are split into two camps (red and white) in grade order and compete for their faction.

Mid-winter Training (Kangeiko)	Judoka train very early in the morning at the coldest time of the year as part of their character training, usually for thirty days.
Mid-summer Training (Shochugeiko)	Same as for the mid-winter training but at the hottest time of the year.
National Championships	Once a year a no-weight category championship is held.

The traditional objectives or purposes of Judo as defined by Jigoro Kano are three:

1. Judo is a method of combat (shobuho)
2. a form of physical training (tai-ikuho) and
3. a form of ethical or character training (shushinho)

Modern Judo

Modern Judo, as it is practised all over the world, is almost entirely free-fighting Judo and it is this which has developed into the sport of Judo. Some national Judo organisations make the learning of Kata part of the requirements for promotion to higher grades, but these are not often introduced before the Black belt stage. Otherwise it is left to the individual to learn Kata if he wishes.

Most Judoka do Judo because of the interest, exercise and self-training they get from free-fighting. Many do Judo as a sport, which is to say their main objective is to become a Judo champion and win medals. Although there is a whole structure from national to international to Olympic Judo championships, contest Judomen are relatively few in number compared with the people at club level who do Judo because they like doing it or for more traditional reasons. Judo thus is a multi-purpose activity.

In free-fighting Judo, the Judoman tries to score by any one of four methods. These are:

1. to throw the opponent cleanly on his back,
2. to hold him on his back for thirty seconds,
3. to gain a submission from a strangle,
4. to gain a submission from an arm (elbow) lock.

Note that no kicks or blows are allowed and that the only joint-lock allowed is on the elbow. Within these four scoring methods the range of technique is enormous. In club training the Judoka polishes up his technique, scoring as often as he can, but in competition it is only necessary to score once, finishing the match there and then. Judo's sudden-death method of scoring is based on the old idea that such a score would be decisive in real combat – a bit like a knockout in boxing.

Judomen fight wearing a traditional Judo suit (Judogi) (see Fig. 1) on a mat which is just about soft enough to fall on but hard enough to move fast on. No shoes are worn.

Fig. 1   Judogi

Modern sport Judo is usually fought in weight categories and under International Judo Federation rules (see Appendix). The present IJF weight categories are:

Under 60 kg
Under 65 kg
Under 71 kg
Under 78 kg
Under 86 kg
Under 95 kg
Over 95 kg

A winning score (ippon) is counted as 10 points, and scores of 7 (Waza-ari), 5 (Yuko) and 3 (Koka) are given depending on how near to the full score they are. An Olympic Gold Medal, for example, can be won on a 3-point score. In addition, where there are infringements of the rules, scores against a fighter of 3 (Shido), 5 (Chui), 7 (Keikoku) and 10 (Hansokumake) can be given.

Ability in Judo is denoted by the colour of the belt the Judoka wears. The traditional colours are:

6th Kyu (grade)	White belt
5th Kyu	White belt
4th Kyu	White belt
3rd Kyu	Brown belt
2nd Kyu	Brown belt
1st Kyu	Brown belt
1st Dan	Black belt
2nd Dan	Black belt
3rd Dan	Black belt
4th Dan	Black belt
5th Dan	Black Belt
6th Dan	Red and White belt
7th Dan	Red and White belt
8th Dan	Red and White belt
9th Dan	Red belt
10th Dan	Red belt

The Kyu (pronounced queue) grades are the novice grades, while the Dan grades imply a degree of mastery. The top fighting grade is about 5th Dan and thereafter grades are given for services to Judo. In the history of Judo only ten men have been promoted to 10th Dan. All have been Japanese.

In Europe and other parts of the world the novice Kyu grades are often in the following colour order: white, yellow, orange, green, blue, brown then 1st to 10th Dan as above.

Grades are mainly obtained by beating other people of the same grade in competition. In addition demonstration of certain techniques or Kata may be required.

2
Basic Judo

Starting and learning Judo

In Judo you have to learn to beat anyone, no matter how big or small. The feel of a throw varies considerably depending upon the size of the opponent in relation to oneself, and this means you must practise your throws on as many different sized people as possible. The best way to do this is to join a Judo club. The next best thing would be to get a small group of interested friends together to learn. Failing this a lot can be learned if just two of you get together.

It is possible to learn a limited amount of Judo entirely on your own. First, a clear mental picture of the technique must be gained, next the move can be practised in front of a mirror, and finally some inanimate object can be used to move against. Perhaps the best thing in this case would be to obtain a wrestler's training dummy or a tall heavy sack and practise hurling it to the ground. Or else a Judo belt can be looped round a tree at about shoulder height and the various footwork and entry moves could be practised. Indeed this method of training against a tree was one of the favourite training methods of the great Kimura, many times All-Japan champion.

If you are learning your Judo outside a proper club and without an experienced instructor you will need to wear some strong and loosefitting garment which can withstand a lot of pushing and pulling, and, of course, some softish surface on which to take falls is required. Mattresses of some sort would be all right for falling on but a much harder surface is required for moving around on in free-fighting. If the training surface is too soft and dumpy there is a risk of twisted ankles and knees. Since there is a potential risk in all the Judo moves, great caution must be exercised in the early stages. When trying free-fighting for the first few times, deliberately slow it down, relax and do not be too keen to win. Above all, relax.

When joining a club, check that it belongs to an organisation recognised by the International Judo Federation. This is the body that controls Judo at world and Olympic levels. In any particular country check with your national Olympic association to find which body it deals with for Olympic Judo and this will be the recognised one. In Britain for example, the British Judo Association is the body recognised by the British Olympic Association.

When joining a club you will first be shown how to fall properly and then gradually introduced to the techniques of free-fighting. It is not necessary to be super-fit to start Judo. The limited amount of relaxed Judo you will do at the beginning will gradually condition you for the longer periods of faster fighting. The club will provide all the equipment you need or will tell you how to get it.

Since there are different ways to approach Judo it might be necessary to shop around to find the instructor who teaches the sort of Judo you want to learn. Whatever approach is adopted, at some point the Judo has to be realistically tested in Randori (free-fighting) or in contest. If you want to know how good your prospective instructor is, watch his students in free-fighting or contest. If you see a lot of strong-arm mauling going on, look elsewhere. On the other hand, if you see dainty, non-physical, almost dance-like free-fighting, also beware. Good Judo is fast, energetic, clean and decisive with lots of big fast throws. When choosing your instructor, also make sure that he belongs to a recognised Judo organisa-ion.

Judo for everybody

Judo is a vigorous activity but it is practised by the young and the not so young of both sexes. However, depending upon your sex, age and aims there are slightly differing ways to approach Judo.

For the not so young, Judo can be surprisingly heavy exercise. Get your doctor to give you a check-up before your first session. If you have any back or knee problems Judo may well aggravate them unless you are very careful. If you have no ailments of any sort do not hesitate to try Judo. A good instructor will introduce you gradually to the full-blooded thing and you will quickly find yourself getting fitter and fitter. It is not necessary to 'get fit' before you take it up. If you find that you have been plunged in at the deep end do not hesitate to ask the instructor if you can rest or change partners if you happen to have a rough one. A good instructor will know your limits. If you find that you are not allowed to go at your own pace look elsewhere for a less vigorous session.

If you are allowed to pace yourself do what you can the first time then gradually try to do more and more on subsequent sessions. A proper beginners' course will consist mostly of instruction with a little bit of free-fighting. As you get towards the end of the course and move into the club sessions proper the ratio changes and you will find yourself doing mainly free-fighting. This is when you must learn to pace yourself.

Women who do Judo fall into three main categories. Those who do it for competitive purposes (women's championships etc.) will or should be doing exactly the same as their male counterparts. The majority who do it for recreational reasons must watch who they train with. There are some women-only sessions but the majority of sessions are mixed. Training with other women is usually safe enough as it is with the instructors and high grades. To be avoided are the clumsy beginners and lower grades. Sometimes they are not aware of their own strength in relation to women. Do not hesitate to end a practice with someone if you think he or she is dangerous.

A leotard is probably the best clothing for women under their Judo suits. Tee-shirts tend to ride up during a hectic session. The recreational woman Judo player will find herself doing less strenuous Judo than the men. Experience will show what throws are easier to do. Groundwork presents no problems.

Those women who do Judo for self-defence purposes should note the safety and other hints above and read the chapter on self-defence.

Many children now do Judo. Seven years old is about the youngest starting age although some clubs will not take students before ten. Very young ones are not allowed to do arm-locks or strangles. There is a danger that they might injure each other on the mat or others outside the club. The instructor or parent must stress that Judo must be confined to the club mat. Strict discipline must be observed in this respect. With the very young ones the onus is on the instructor to take full safety precautions. All high throws must be carefully supervised. Judo is, however, a fairly rough and tumble activity so a few knocks cannot be avoided.

Attitudes to strangles and arm-locks vary considerably. Many instructors will not allow their juniors to do them before their sixteenth birthday. Others introduce them to their juniors much earlier. Junior competitions make clear whether they are allowed and if so from what age. Currently in the British Judo Association arm-locks and strangles are not allowed in competition and Randori under fourteen years of age. This is not to say that they cannot be shown in instruction below that age. It is largely left to the discretion of the instructor. Parents must satisfy themselves how strict the discipline is in relation to these techniques in a club.

Parents should avoid introducing their child to over-crowded sessions or to clubs that have mats close to dangerous projections and sharp edges. Observation will show how safety conscious the instructor is. If he is not, have a word with him or remove your child.

Hygiene

Personal hygiene is important in Judo. Your Judo suit must be kept clean and white. A few good sessions will quickly saturate your suit with sweat and if not cleaned, it will quickly start to smell unpleasantly. A clean white suit is demanded not only for hygienic reasons but also for aesthetic ones. A white Judo suit is part of the 'image' of Judo.

Finger and toe nails must also be kept short. Long and ragged nails may quickly get broken off or scratch the other person. Long, big, toe nails are especially to be watched as these can make deep cuts on your opponent's ankles when you try ankle-throws and similar foot-throws.

Before you leave the changing room, make sure that you wash your feet. This will help to avoid any unpleasant smells and keep the mat clean. Any foot infections must be treated instantly and covered if training is to continue. For serious infections training must stop till the infection clears up.

Rings and other metallic objects must not be worn as these may injure others. If rings cannot be removed they may be taped over.

Dojo problems

Other minor problems may occur in the early days of your Judo. Stubbed toes and bruised shins are common among beginners. These come about from foot throws when the beginner, instead of listening carefully to what the instructor says, starts to kick out at the opponent's ankles. Note carefully the various positions for your feet in these throws, make the throws carefully and you can avoid this common complaint.

Mat-burns may also occur when you do free-fighting. These come about when a part of the body is dragged or rubbed on the mat, leaving a small graze. This may be because the mat is too rough or because your Judo suit is too short or because you are making a wrong movement. Frequently you may get rubbed on the same spot more than once. If you can identify the cause of the graze you will be able to take steps to avoid it. Putting plasters over them may temporarily ease the pain but they soon get ripped off. Unless the graze gets really raw, carry on training and soon you will find that they will disappear for good.

A raw neck is another similar complaint. When the opponent pulls on your jacket it rubs the back of the neck and may cause soreness. A new judo suit is often the cause. Powder or some sort of towelling around the neck may ease the pain but eventually you will find that it will disappear as your neck gets used to it.

As with any other new physical activity it is quite likely that you will feel stiff after your first few Judo sessions. Judo is an all-round physical exercise and you will find muscles aching that you did not know existed. After three or four sessions you should find the stiffness disappearing.

For more serious injuries see the chapter on contest Judo.

Having actually started Judo, bear in mind the old Judo saying that a throw must be practised three thousand times before it becomes effective. This is perhaps an exaggeration but what it says is – you will need to practise and practise and keep on practising till the moves become an automatic part of you. Judo is not just a collection of 'tricks' learned in five minutes.

How to fall properly

The Japanese with their love of training slogans coined the phrase, 'Ukemi Sannen' which means 'three years (must be spent) on breakfalls'. Much of one's Judo life is spent throwing and being thrown, but with many people the fear of being thrown is uppermost; consequently much of their time is spent negatively trying not to be thrown, instead of concentrating on throwing the opponent. However, the Japanese believe that with a lot of practice in breakfalling the fear of being thrown can be overcome so that one can work more positively on one's attack. There are one or two exercises that *prepare* you for the real throw and these will be described shortly. Bear in mind that learning to fall properly is not something you must spend months learning to the exclusion of all else. All the types of scoring techniques should be tried from lesson one, with breakfalling taking a progressively shorter time as you improve.

The breakfall   (Ukemi)
For the opponent to score in Judo he must throw you on your back – and this is the best part of the body to land on. You may be somersaulted forwards or toppled backwards, but in whichever direction you are thrown, there are three simple rules:

1.   Let your back take the fall.
2.   Tuck your chin in, keeping your head off the mat.
3.   Beat the mat hard with your free arm the moment your back touches the mat.

Fig. 2   Breakfall   Fig. 3   Breakfall

Tucking in the chin prevents the head whiplashing back into the mat on impact, and beating the mat lessens the impact of the throw.

    Points two and three can be practised by first squatting down (Fig. 2) then rolling backwards keeping the chin tucked in and striking the mat with one or both arms the moment the shoulder-blades touch the mat (Fig. 3). Note the angle of the beating arm to the body. Practise this movement slowly to start with, then more and more vigorously. The next stage is to start from a standing position, collapsing in a relaxed manner through the squatting position, then beating the mat exactly as before. Note that when the arm hits the mat, the palm of the hand slaps the mat too.

One other method of practising the fall, before you take the real thing, is the forward rolling breakfall. This is like the gymnastic forward roll, except that it is done not squarely to the front but diagonally across the back.

Fig. 4   Forward roll   Fig. 5   Forward roll

From a standing position take a step forward, reaching out with the right hand down to the mat about two feet in front of the right foot (Fig. 4). Tuck your head in close to the body, then roll forward with the area of the right shoulder-blade making first contact with the mat. Continue the rolling movement right the way through (Fig. 5) so that it takes you back up on to your feet. The faster this movement is done from the standing position the easier it is to roll up completely on to the feet. Practise this breakfall more and more vigorously on both sides (that is, starting with left foot and arm forward). When you have mastered this, practise it over a kneeling body. This type of breakfall is only done from certain throws, but it is a good exercise to get you used to turning forward into the mat.

It only takes a few minutes to learn the elements of the breakfall, but a bit longer to relax when going over and perfecting the timing of the arm beat. The best way to learn this is to be thrown as many times as possible, first on a soft surface such as a crashmat, then gradually on to a proper mat. Get a training partner to throw you with as many different throws as possible, on both left and right sides (for explanation of left and right sides in throwing see the section on gripping).

One natural reaction of most beginners when taking a Judo throw for the first few times is to try to reach out to the mat with their hands, as they are about to hit it. This is like a learner skater who, when sliding over backwards on to the seat of his pants, puts both arms down behind himself to cushion the fall. When a throw is done fast in Judo there is a danger that the arms can be damaged if they get caught under the falling body, so not only does the beating of the mat disperse a certain amount of the shock of the fall but it gives the arms something safe to do.

Another common fault with beginners when on the receiving end of throws is to anticipate the throw and to start to turn into the direction of the throw. What then happens is that the beginner gets *over-thrown*.

The thrower, expecting his partner's body to be in a certain position, makes the appropriate moves to put his partner on his back, but if, when he is moving in for the throw, his partner starts to turn in the direction he is expecting to fall, the relative positioning will be wrong, so that instead of landing on his back, the partner may end up being thrown on one shoulder or even on to his stomach.

The best advice when being thrown, especially when practising the breakfalls, is to simply do nothing. Just stand there and let your partner make his moves, neither resisting, nor moving, nor crumpling up. Part of every Judo session should be throwing practice, in which not only can one practise one's throws against a non-resisting partner but sharpen up one's breakfalls too.

How to grip

Most Judo throws are done by holding the opponent's jacket. The rules allow a hold to be taken almost anywhere on the Judo suit or body (see Appendix on IJF rules) but there is one main limitation. Apart from the standard hold described below, the other holds can only be maintained for as long as it takes to make an attack, which is estimated to be about three to four seconds. Thus, for example, you can hold the trousers at the knee to make an attack, but no longer than about four seconds.

In the *standard hold*, one hand grips one side of the jacket above the belt and the other hand the other side of the jacket above the belt. For a right-handed person, the usual hold is: right hand holding the lapel about own shoulder-height and left hand holding the sleeve at the elbow (Fig. 6). This standard hold is best because the wide grip enables you to turn your opponent's body, which must be done with all the throws that pitch him forward (otherwise he would land on his face) and also because it immobilises one of his arms. This sleeve-lapel grip is the one which will enable you to do the greatest number of throws.

Fig. 6   Standard Hold

Note: all moves in this book are described for right-handed people. In the case of left-handers, substitute right for left and vice versa in all cases. From a right-handed grip the thrower should make a right-sided attack, which is to say, he turns in an anti-clockwise direction, bringing the right side of his body closer to the opponent.

Variations on the standard hold are: holding both sleeves or holding both lapels, but the sleeve-lapel grip is the one most strongly recommended.

When holding the opponent's jacket, gather the cloth in with the sleeve grip so that the arm inside moves when the jacket is pulled, not just the jacket. Bear in mind that the aim is not to throw the jacket but the man inside it. Thus the opponent should be lightly but firmly controlled between your two gripping hands, with his jacket pulled across his back, not left slack.

In the chapter on throws you will see that the grip differs slightly from throw to throw. Note these differences carefully.

How to move around the mat

In free-fighting, whether attacking or defending, a lot of movement around the mat is involved. Indeed your very stance greatly affects your chances of success or failure. Jigoro Kano, the inventor of Judo, regarded correct stance as so important that he made it one of his three central principles of Judo. The correct Judo stance is known as Shizentai or Natural Posture. It is an upright stance with the feet about shoulder width apart, and whether attacking or defending, this stance should be maintained as much as possible.

To a beginner this rule may not seem very important, but if time is taken out to observe inexperienced people in Randori, you will see that the natural tendency when fighting is to crouch and spread the legs. The crouching defensive stance, known as Jigotai in Japanese, suffers from two main defects. First, mobility is reduced, which means it is not a good position to attack from, and secondly, it is not such a good defensive position as it seems. It is better to stay upright and move out of the way of attacks than to sink into this sitting-duck position.

On the other hand, watch two experts fight and you will notice how straight they stand, whether attacking or defending.

The general rule is to keep the back straight and the head up, and to move around with the feet always about shoulder width apart. If the feet come close together there is a loss of stability. This is very obvious, for example, when the feet are pressed close together. Wide-spread feet lead to loss of mobility and feet close together lead to loss of stability. The ideal position is in between, about shoulder-width apart.

When moving around, move in a somewhat relaxed manner, keeping the feet close to the ground.

3

Throws

The main emphasis in traditional and modern Judo is on throwing. Although the Kata include kicks and punches, the stress in Judo as a fighting system is on throwing the opponent down hard and fast.

There are various types of throw. The traditional classification is as follows: arm-throws (Te-waza), hip-throws (Koshi-waza), leg-throws (Ashi-waza), front sacrifice-throws (Ma-sutemi-waza) and side sacrifice-throws (Yoko-sutemi-waza). In addition there are counter-throws (Kaeshi-waza) and take-downs, which are moves which roll the opponent to the ground rather than throw him down, and are used by groundwork specialists.

To be considered effective, a throw has to be fast and the opponent must land more or less squarely on his back with some force.

The traditional list of throws (the Gokyo) includes forty throws, but the late Kyuzo Mifune, 10th Dan, in his book *The Way and Techniques*, adds another twenty-two. In addition, there are usually slightly differing ways to do any single throw.

Despite the great number of throws, contest statistics, which have been kept for some time in Japan and lately in the West, indicate a small group of throws which consistently score in major competition. The following ten throws, for example, account for over eighty per cent of all throwing scores in every competition. The figures following the throws indicate how many times that throw scored out of a total of 512 scores made in three consecutive world championships.

Morote Seoinage (double-arm shoulder-throw)	88
Uchi-mata (inner thigh-throw)	76
Osoto-gari (major outer reaping)	71
O-uchi-gari (major inner reaping)	43
Tai-otoshi (body-drop)	43
Harai-goshi (sweeping hip)	35
Kosoto-gari (minor outer reaping)	31
Kouchi-gari (minor inner reaping)	25
Ippon Seoinage (one-arm shoulder-throw)	16
Tsuri-komi-ashi (propping drawing ankle)	11

In this book twenty throws are described, including all the above. Some of the throws are more difficult to learn than others (Uchi-mata for example), but all will repay diligent study and practise.

Learning to throw a good opponent takes some time. Throws are not meant to be done crudely, using a lot of muscle to take the man over, but should be exact, precise movements which have to be constantly refined so as to fell stronger and more experienced opposition. Concentrate on accuracy of position and timing – never be content to muscle somebody over.

Although the throws are described sectionally, it is important to remember that any throw takes a second or two at the most to accomplish, and that all the footwork, armwork and bodywork merge into each other with no interruption of movement. Most throws are a brief explosion.

Osoto-gari (major outer reaping)

Of the first five big scorers, this is the only throw which sends the opponent backwards. Perhaps the reason that rear-throws do not score so much (compared with forward-throws) is because the opponent can usually move back as fast as the thrower can move forward. However, the statistics indicate that this is a big scorer. Often it is used as a counter-throw and here it scores a lot (see the chapter on counter-throws).

The mechanics of this throw are simple, and therefore it is often one of the first throws taught to beginners. However, doing it on a moving opponent presents some problems. For maximum success, beginners are advised to concentrate on the *opportunity* for the throw.

Opportunity
One of the best moments for this throw is when the opponent has moved

or is moving his right leg towards you. Whether done statically or on the move, it is necessary to align yourself closely and squarely in front of this right leg at the start of the movement. The smaller the gap you have to cross the better.

Grip
The thrower's right hand grips the lapel about level with the opponent's collar-bone. The left hand holds over the opponent's right arm, grasping the area of cloth between the lapel and the sleeve (Fig. 7).

Fig. 7   O-soto-gari   Fig. 8   O-soto-gari

Footwork
Take a short step forward with the left foot to a point about level with the opponent's right foot but about six inches away. Balancing on this left foot, swing your right leg through the gap (Fig. 8) beyond the opponent's right leg, then reap strongly back into it, connecting with the back of your right knee on the back of his knee, and sweep his leg clear of the ground.

Armwork
As you step forward with the left foot, bear down with your left arm on the opponent's right arm, pushing the opponent over so that he is rocking backwards on his right heel. Your right arm works with the left in pushing the opponent off-balance on to his right heel. A strong action of the right arm, working with a strong action of the right leg, is vital in this throw.

Bodywork

Until the start of the reaping action, the body moves straight towards the opponent, making chest contact. Once the sweep or reap is under way, make sure that your upper body swings down towards the mat as your right leg sweeps back and up. Think of the reap as being done not with just the leg but with the whole body in a see-saw movement – head down, leg up (Fig. 9).

Fig. 9   O-soto-gari

The movements of this throw are simple, yet it takes time to be able to bring it off in contest. To gain best results from it, concentrate on launching your attack when the opponent's right leg is near you – the nearer the better.

Morote Seoinage   (double-arm shoulder-throw)

This throw heads the list of top-scoring throws. It requires rather more effort than most of the other throws. Until the armwork is mastered, some discomfort can be felt in the arms and shoulders. Once mastered, however, it enables a lighter man to throw a much heavier one. It is a difficult throw to do on someone shorter than yourself. When learning the throw, it helps to think of it as a 'back-throw'. Indeed, Seoi (pronounced say-oy) means to 'carry on the back' and not 'shoulder', although the latter is the common English translation. Thus when you make the throw, concentrate on getting your back squarely touching the opponent's front. When this is done the thrower will be fully in front of, and blocking, the forward movement of the opponent.

Opportunity

This throw can be attempted in most situations. The best opportunity perhaps is when the opponent is leaning forward somewhat, bending from the waist with straight arms.

Grip

Take hold with the right hand about the height of the opponent's chest. It is important to have a lot of cloth to move around. On the other hand, do not hold too low with the right hand, as this can indicate your intention to the opponent. The left hand holds the sleeve at the elbow.

Footwork

From a face-on position to the opponent, the thrower has to turn completely round. The footwork for this must be made exact and automatic. Step forward and across with your foot placing it down near the opponent's right foot. Place your weight on the right foot and using this as a pivot, swing the left foot back and round to a position near the opponent's left foot. Keep the weight on the balls of the feet and make these actions bouncy and light.

Fig. 10   Morote-seoi-nage

Armwork

As you step in and the body turns, pull strongly forward and up with your left arm, and retaining the grip on the opponent's left lapel, fold your right arm as you swing your elbow under his right arm-pit (Fig. 10). The feel of this throw is as if you were swinging a heavy sack on to your back.

Bodywork

Once the feet and arms are in position (Fig. 11) finish off the throw by curling the upper body down towards the mat. If some resistance is met with, it may be necessary to straighten the legs so as to lift the opponent up before you finish the throw (Fig. 12). As you curl forward, the action will unload the opponent off your back.

Fig. 11   Morote-seoi-nage

Fig. 12   Morote-seoi-nage

When finishing, curl tightly down towards your own feet. Try to avoid an undirected heave up in the air. The throw succeeds when the opponent's back touches the mat – and that is where your efforts end.

If the armwork is done too slowly, the opponent will stiffen his arms, making it difficult for you to get them into place. Concentrate on exploding into position, making your footwork and armwork as fast as possible. Once this has been done, the thrower is in a very strong position indeed and can usually complete the throw, no matter how the opponent wriggles.

Ippon Seoinage (one-arm shoulder-throw)

This is the shoulder-throw that is usually taught to beginners, probably because it is more comfortable to do. It is, however, more difficult to score Ippon (10-point winning score) with it compared with the previous Morote Seoinage, and the statistics show this.

Grip
The left hand hold has to be very secure. If your left hand is strong, hold the sleeve near the elbow, or take hold over the opponent's right arm, gathering as much sleeve and lapel as possible at the level of the opponent's right arm-pit.

Opportunity
The throw may be done against an opponent who is moving either forward or backwards, and, of course, standing still. But it does not work so well against a circling opponent. It can be done against an upright or a crouching stance, but probably it is more used against the latter.

Footwork
The entry footwork is standard, that is the right foot moves diagonally about a foot in front of the left foot; then pivoting on this right foot, the left foot is brought round to a comfortable distance away from it – about one foot. This is virtually the same footwork as for the previous version of shoulder-throw. As the legs swing round into position, the legs must be bent so that the thrower feels he is getting lower than his opponent.

Armwork
As you move your feet into position, drop the right grip and swing the right arm under the opponent's right arm-pit. The exact position for this is with your right biceps under the arm-pit (*not* the top of the shoulder near your neck). Pull forward and down with the left hand and punch up with your right fist, and this will make a very tight grip on the opponent's right arm. The throw will not succeed unless you securely trap this arm.

Bodywork
Once you have moved your feet and arms into position, push your right hip out further to the side so that any forward movement by the opponent is blocked (Fig. 13).

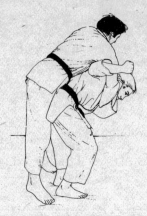

Fig. 13   Ippon seoi-nage

Finish

Shoulder-throw is traditionally classified as an arm-throw, which means that a lot of emphasis is on the action of the arms. Once into position the arms must continue their strong forward pulling action over and down to the mat. Curl the upper body downwards, straighten the legs, twist slightly round to the left foot and off-load the opponent from your back and right shoulder.

Think of throwing your opponent to his right-front- corner (see section on throwing directions). Get your pull going in that direction right from the start of the throw and keep the whole throw moving in that direction.

Seoi-otoshi   (shoulder drop)

One of the difficulties of shoulder-throws is to position yourself low enough, especially if you are taller than your opponent. This variation of shoulder-throw is one good solution to the problem. The armwork for it can be either that used for the one-arm shoulder-throw or for the double-arm shoulder-throw, but here I will describe the latter and with a spin-turn entry. It is important to distinguish between the two types of foot-work when making a throw which requires a turn-around action. The normal or standard method is to position the right foot, then pivot on it as you swing round into position. In the rarer spin-turn footwork, it is the left foot which is positioned and which is used as a pivot to swing the body round. The whole action is much more of an obvious spin than the standard footwork and is usually called the 'spin-turn'.

Grip
The left hand holds the sleeve and the right hand holds low on the lapel at about the height of the opponent's chest.

Opportunity
The throw is often done to an opponent who is square on or who has his right leg and right side pulled back (as in the case of left-handers).

Footwork
Move the right leg back about a foot and bring your left foot over to where your right foot was. Transfer your weight to the ball of the foot and, lifting your right knee high, swing your leg (foot leading) through the gap between the two bodies, pivoting on the left foot and turning the body round. Continue the spin, taking your legs into a low fencing-like lunge position, with your right leg placed directly across and back and touching the opponent's shins. It is this drop into the lunge position that enables a taller man to get very low.

Armwork
From the very start of the throw pull strongly forward and up with your left arm; then, as the footwork spins you into position, fold the right arm under the opponent's right arm-pit.

Fig. 14   Seoi-otoshi

Finish

When finally in position (Fig. 14) complete the throw by straightening the legs, which will lift the opponent up, and curl forward and down to the mat with the upper body.

Uchi-mata (inner thigh)

This throw is most often brought off against an opponent who is crouching or whose legs are fairly wide apart. Perhaps this is one of the reasons that Uchi-mata scores so often in competition, for the crouching stance is a very common contest position. Once the thrower is in position with his lifting leg between his opponent's legs, there is very little that can stop that lift, short of a low ceiling!

Grip

Hold high on the opponent's collar with the right hand and low on his sleeve. This grip with the right hand which is almost round the back of the opponent's neck, will control his head, which is important for this throw.

Stance

The grip above will bring you somewhat right side on to the opponent,

Fig. 15   Uchi-mata

with your right leg forward (Fig. 15). When practising this get your opponent to spread his legs and bend forward from the waist.

Footwork
Pivoting on the forward right foot, bring your left foot sharply round close behind it, placing it on the ground about one foot in front of the opponent's feet, but directly in the middle (Fig. 16). The pivoting action of the foot will have brought you round so as to face the same way as your opponent. Your left foot should now be pointing in the same direction as his two feet. With no break in the movement, transfer your weight to the left foot and sweep your right leg up between his two legs, making contact at the top of the opponent's left inside thigh. Continue this sweep so that he is lifted up into the air, (Fig. 17) both feet clear of the mat. Stretch the sweeping right leg to its maximum and point the toes.

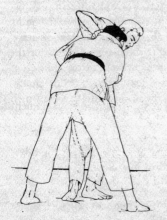

Fig. 16   Uchi-mata

Fig. 17   Uchi-mata

Armwork
As the legs move into position but before you begin the sweep with the right leg, pull strongly forward with both arms pulling the opponent's chest into contact with the right lower side of your own chest. Lift the right elbow up into the air.

Finish
To gain maximum lift with the right leg, drop the upper body down

to the mat and twist round to your left. The higher the leg can lift the better, and it will not be able to do this unless the upper body drops down to the mat in a see-saw action. The left hand, which started off by holding low on the opponent's right sleeve, now comes into play. As you drop your head down to the mat, pull strongly with the left hand down towards your left hip. This has the effect of unloading the opponent off your right leg and dropping him to the mat.

Uchi-mata II

In the previous description of Uchi-mata, the standard entry footwork was described, and this works well on a static opponent or one circling in a clockwise direction. However, should the opponent be circling the other way (round to your left) it becomes quite easy to miss the throw altogether, leaving you open for a counter-throw (see chapter on counter-throws). When the opponent does move in this direction the following variation of Uchi-mata works very well. It also works well against a static opponent. The footwork for this variation is the spin-turn. One advantage of the spin-turn is that the attack to the opponent comes from a different angle. A normal attack is straight at the opponent through his defending arms, but the spin-turn enables an attack to be made from the side, which often catches an opponent by surprise.

Grip
Take the standard hold: right hand holding lapel about own shoulder-height and left hand holding the sleeve fairly low down.

Opportunity
When practising this throw, start on a static opponent whose legs are slightly wider than shoulder-width apart. When you have got used to the movement, practise on an opponent circling to your left (anti-clockwise). The feel of the throw is that one is at the centre of the circle and that the opponent is moving, or being moved, round the perimeter.

Footwork
From a square-on stance, move your right foot back about one foot and instantly bring your left foot over to occupy the space where the right foot was. Place the weight on the ball of the left foot and lift the right leg up high (Fig. 18).

Fig. 18   Uchi-mata II

Fig. 19   Uchi-mata II

Armwork
As the feet move into position, pull the opponent strongly forward, i.e. to where you were before you made the initial steps.

Finish
Having raised your right leg high, swing it through the gap between the two bodies and then back up between the opponent's two legs, aiming for the top of the left thigh. As the right leg swings into position, twist your body strongly round to the left, head going down towards the mat, and fall away from the opponent. Pull strongly all the while with your left hand round towards your left hip. Lift as high as you can with the right leg.

Up to three-quarters of the way through this throw, it will feel as if the thrower will merely collapse in a heap on the mat with the opponent on top of him, but if he holds on tight and persists with the grip and lifting right leg, the opponent will be suddenly spun off his feet (Fig. 19).

The whole throw is a fairly complicated spinning and twisting movement, but if mastered will pay big dividends in competition. If done very fast the thrower will often spin right over the opponent after he has landed on the mat and land on the mat himself. This does not matter since it is only the first man to hit the mat from a throw who loses points.

Harai-goshi   (sweeping hip)

This throw is often done by the bigger, heavier man. Quite often the thrower will fall to the mat on completing this throw. In this case, it is called Harai-makikomi. As a general rule, it is recommended that all throws should be done with the thrower keeping his balance. With this throw however, it happens that the thrower, sensing that he has almost toppled his opponent, will throw his weight down to the mat (holding on tightly to the opponent); it is in this situation that having that extra weight is an advantage. If the lighter man wants to succeed with this throw, he must concentrate on explosive arm and leg work.

Grip
Hold round the neck at the back of the opponent's collar with your right hand. This is needed to control his head. Take a strong grip with your left hand on the sleeve. The action of the left arm in this throw is very important and so the grip must be very secure (Fig. 20).

Fig. 20   Harai-goshi

Fig. 21   Harai-goshi

Footwork
Move your right foot forward and slightly across, transfer your weight to it, and swing your left foot round behind. This will have swung your body round so that it is almost facing the same direction as the opponent's.

Transfer your weight to the left foot and using your right leg, sweep up into the opponent's right thigh (Fig. 21).

Armwork
As your legs move into position, pull the opponent strongly forward off-balance but concentrate the pull more strongly in your left arm so that the opponent is unbalanced to his right front corner. Try to pull him forward so that his chest makes contact with the right side of your chest.

Finish
The throw is finished by sweeping the opponent vigorously up into the air with the right leg. As you do this, dip the upper body down to the mat in the see-saw action and twist round to the left. This will spin the opponent over your thigh and drop him to the mat (Fig. 22).

Fig. 22   Harai-goshi

Points to concentrate on in this throw are:

1. a strong pull with the left hand
2. making chest contact, and
3. a vigorous sweep up with the right leg.

Harai-goshi is a hip-throw and it must be remembered that the opponent is not lifted up with the action of the right leg alone but with the aid of the right hip. If 'chest contact' is maintained this will happen naturally.

O-guruma (major wheel)

There are a number of throws in Judo which contain the word 'guruma' in their name and this gives a clue to the throwing action in many of them. Guruma means 'wheel' and indicates any circular, spinning or twisting throwing action. This throw looks very similar to Harai-goshi, but the difference lies in the final action. In Harai-goshi, the right leg sweeps into the opponent's right leg, trying to move it and the rest of his body, but in O-guruma the thrower's right leg acts more as a static block and the thrower seeks to twist his opponent over it, using his whole body in a large twisting action.

This throw can be very spectacular and it is said to be one way that a smaller man can throw a considerably bigger man. A lot of power can be generated from the spin-turn entry.

Grip
The grip is the standard one: left hand on the sleeve, right hand on the lapel at about own shoulder-height.

Opportunity
The throw is often done against an opponent who is moving diagonally forward to your left side or who is circling in an anti-clockwise direction in relation to the thrower. The opponent may be straight or crouching.

Footwork
It is normal in Judo free-fighting for the thrower's footwork to parallel the opponent's footwork. If this did not happen, feet and knees would collide, since both parties are standing and moving close to each other as in ballroom dancing. If the opponent moves diagonally forward, then one moves diagonally backwards, and if he circles one way, then one circles the opposite way and so on.

If, however, one party suddenly stands still when the other is circling, the latter will move off to the side, and it is this that gives an opportunity for O-guruma. As the opponent circles to your left, suddenly stand still, transfer your weight to the left foot and lift the right leg off the mat (Fig. 23). In the split second it takes to do this, the opponent will have moved off to your left side. Spinning your body round on the left foot, drive your right leg through the gap between the two bodies and position your straight leg across both of the opponent's front lower thighs – just above the knees.

Armwork

As your legs move into position, pull strongly with your arms, especially the left one, and keep the opponent moving along his original direction, that is off to your left side.

Finish

As the right leg spins into position across the opponent's thighs, pull him strongly over your out-stretched blocking right leg, concentrating on the action of your left arm. Drop your upper body down and twist strongly round to your left. The whole (uninterrupted) spin-turn entry and final twist of the body will spin the opponent over your right leg (Fig. 24) and drop him to the mat.

Fig. 23   O-guruma

Fig. 24   O-guruma

O-goshi (major hip)

This is another throw that is often taught to beginners in their first few lessons because it is so easy to do against a non-resisting partner, but problems arise when trying it in free-fighting or contest. Once the thrower is in position, it is an extremely powerful throw and can be used against much heavier people. Anyone wanting to specialise in this throw must concentrate on ways of getting the right arm into position.

Grip

The thrower's grip is the standard right hand on lapel and left hand holding the sleeve. The throw may be done against a crouching or upright opponent.

Footwork

The footwork is the simple standard turn-around footwork. Move the right foot forward and diagonally across to the left, placing it about a foot in front of the left foot. Pivoting on this, swing the left foot back and round, so that both feet are about shoulder-width apart and facing the same direction as the opponent's feet. This will have brought the body right round.

Armwork

As your feet move into position, pull the opponent strongly off-balance to his front, using your left arm, and dropping the right hand grip, snake your right arm down and round the opponent's waist to hold the belt or jacket or both, in the middle of his lower back.

The position of the right arm can vary quite a bit. It can be placed higher up the back nearer the shoulder-blades, or it may not hold at all, but be placed flat on the back (palm-down) without taking the cloth.

Finish

As the right arm and the feet move into position, the thrower must bend his legs and thrust his hips deeply into position, across in front of the opponent's lower stomach (Fig. 25). If the opponent is crouching or leaning forward, try to fit your hips snugly into the angle formed between the trunk and the thighs. To finish off the throw, straighten the legs (this will lift the opponent off the mat) and twisting slightly to your left, swing him over your hips and down to the mat. Pull strongly with your right arm so as to swing him over your right hip.

The knack with this throw is to get the right arm into position. This can be difficult since the opponent, if he has taken a normal grip, will be holding your right arm at the sleeve, and can fairly easily stop you moving it into position. Opportunities to get the right arm in position occur at the start of a contest or Randori, just before both men have taken hold. Instead of taking a normal right-handed lapel grip, the attacker can quickly snake his right arm round the opponent's

Fig. 25   O-goshi

waist instead. Alternatively, the grip can be taken when the opponent has moved in for a turn-around throw (especially if it is a left-handed one). As the opponent moves out from his failed throw, the thrower maintains his grip on the belt and moves in for O-goshi.

There are a number of throws with different names but which are very similar to O-goshi. If the thrower catches his opponent round the neck with his right arm, it is called Koshi-guruma. If he catches the belt in front with his right hand, it is called Tsuri-goshi.

Further variations on the right arm hold include the right arm going over the opponent's left shoulder and down the centre of the back to catch the belt, or round the outside of the opponent's left arm (so as to trap it) and not underneath it, as in the main version.

Tsuri-komi-goshi   (lift-pull hip-throw)

'Tsuri' means to lift up and out, such as a heavy object out of a barrel. The action of the arms in this throw is up and forwards (towards the thrower). Komi refers to the action of the hips and means to go into something. Supple hips and shoulders are required for this throw, since without this suppleness it is difficult to bring the hips into contact with the opponent.

Grip

This throw is often successful when made against a slightly crouching opponent. The thrower can take a standard grip but must make sure that the right arm holds *under* the opponent's left arm.

Footwork

A spin-turn can be used quite effectively for this throw, but here the normal turn-around footwork is described.

Move your right foot forward and across to a point about one foot in front of your left foot. Pivot on the ball of the right foot and swing the left foot round and behind to the left, so that the feet are about one foot apart, inside the opponent's two feet and facing the same direction. As you swing round, bend your legs so as to get lower than the opponent.

Armwork

As the legs swing round, pull the opponent strongly up and forward, bringing his chest into contact with your right side chest. Your left arm should pull his right arm strongly across your chest, and your right elbow must slide up the left side of his chest and under his left arm-pit. Make sure that your right elbow goes under the arm-pit.

Finish

As your feet move into position and the arms pull forward, swivel your hips into position so that the opponent is drawn forward and on to the right hip (Fig. 26). This means pushing your right hip through to your right, so as to completely block any forward move of the opponent. It is this swivelling action which requires loose, supple hips and lower back. To finish the throw, straighten the legs, continue the forward pulling action of the arms, and twist round to your left, dropping the upper body down towards the mat. This will swing the opponent completely over your hips and down to the mat.

Success with this throw depends upon acquiring supple hips, and snaking them quickly into position.

Tai-otoshi (body-drop)

This throw is traditionally classified as an arm-throw (te-waza). This means that the emphasis in the throw is on the action of the arms.

Fig. 26 Tsuri-komi-goshi

One famous Tai-otoshi expert once described the action of legs in this throw as almost an 'after-thought'.

Tai-otoshi is generally regarded as being difficult to counter, which makes it ideal for competition. It can be difficult to get any feel for this by practising on a static partner. Timing and opportunity are all important, and when these combine on the move, the throw is a quick, effortless explosion.

Opportunity
This throw can be made directly to the right side, front and rear of the opponent. Probably the throw to the opponent's right-front-corner is the most common, and this will be described. When done to the right-front-corner, the opponent can be caught as he steps forward with his right foot, when it is level with his other foot, or when it is back. Tai-otoshi against level feet will be described.

Grip
The right hand holds the opponent's lapel at about his collar-bone level (not around his neck which is a common fault). The left hand holds the sleeve at the elbow. This grip must be strong.

Footwork
Step diagonally forward about one foot with the right foot. Place the

weight on the ball of the right foot and, pivoting on this, swing the left leg round and back, not close to the other foot, but about two and a half feet away. Twist the body round to the front as you make the steps. However, be careful not to swing round into close contact with the opponent's body. There should be a gap of about one foot between the two bodies. At this point your weight should be evenly distributed between both feet (Fig. 27).

Armwork

As with all the other throws, the armwork proceeds at the same time as the footwork. Pull strongly forward and up with your left hand, unbalancing the opponent to his right-front-corner. The right arm starts by pulling the opponent forward at the beginning of the throw, but as your footwork swings you round into position, this action changes into a push. The right arm pulls then pushes the opponent forward. The left arm pulls all the way.

Fig. 27 Tai-otoshi

Fig. 28 Tai-otoshi

Finish

Once you have pulled the opponent forward with your arms and pivoted into position, the throw is completed by twisting round to your left (this will tip the opponent on to his right foot) and driving your right leg directly across in front of the opponent's right leg, fitting your right ankle snugly in front of his right ankle (Fig. 28). Your right leg will trip the opponent and the continuation of the twisting action of the body will flip him off his feet.

When making the throw, try to keep the weight on your toes and spring lightly into position. Concentrate on the left arm pull, first taking the opponent forward, then pulling round to your left hip so as to twist him off his feet.

O-uchi-gari   (major inner reaping)

This is a very powerful attack directed against the opponent's legs. Not only does it score well on its own, but works well in combination with other throws (see the section on combination throws).

Opportunity

The standard opportunity for this is when the opponent has spread his feet more than shoulder width apart. This may occur when he has taken a larger step forward or back than usual, or when he is simply bracing back against a threatened front-direction throw. The more sudden the throw is, the better, since it can be completely stopped if the opponent is able to switch his bodyweight off the attacked leg. The closer his feet are, the quicker he can do this, hence the need to attack when the feet are widespread.

Grip

Take the standard grip on the lapel at own chest height and on the sleeve at the elbow. The opponent spreads his legs very wide.

Armwork

The action of the arms is uncomplicated. Push obliquely down behind the opponent, aiming the knuckles at a spot on the mat five feet behind him. This oblique angle is important. Do not push horizontally backwards. The push down with both arms must be done very abruptly.

Footwork

Turning very slightly right side on to your opponent, advance the right foot about six inches then bring your left foot close in behind it. Next lunge forward with your right leg (driving off your left), insert it between the opponent's legs (Fig. 29) then hook his left leg forward and away, making contact between your right calf and his left calf.

Finish

The sudden push back with the arms and the hooking forward of the opponent's left leg must coincide. This will start to stagger him backwards. Continue the throw by twisting slightly round to your *right*, and throw your bodyweight into the opponent. As he topples backwards follow him down to the ground (Fig. 30), being careful not to actually crash on top of him. Your right foot must not touch the ground for support at any point in the hooking action.

Fig. 29   O-uchi-gari

Fig. 30   O-uchi-gari

A common fault is to lift the opponent's left leg up in the air when making the hooking action. This is wrong. Make sure that this leg is pulled forward and not lifted. If you think of skimming the toes of your right foot along the ground as you make the hooking action, this will prevent you from lifting the opponent's leg.

One of the features of this throw, when used in combination with another throw, is that the opponent will deliberately lift his leg up to avoid the attack, but this then gives you an opportunity to catch the lifted leg or attack the other leg.

Ko-uchi-gari   (minor inner reaping)

The action of this throw is very similar to the previous one, being an attack between the opponent's legs, especially when he has them spread wider than usual. However, in this case it is the opponent's right leg that is being attacked.

It is a very fast throw and can be suddenly used with great effect in free-fighting or contest. It also works well in combination with other throws.

Opportunity

There are two main opportunities for this throw – the static and moving one. When it is done on the move, the thrower starts to attack the opponent's right leg as it steps forward. A split second before the foot actually touches the ground, the leg is hooked forward. The effect of this is that of somebody taking a big step forward on to a patch of ice, then having the foot skid away forwards.

When it is done statically, which is just as good an opportunity as the moving one, the opponent should have his legs spread wider than shoulder-width, preferably with his right leg forward and left leg back (Fig. 31). The opponent may make a longer than normal step forward or he may be induced to do so by subtle pulling pressure with your left arm. Alternatively, if you move faster round the mat than your partner wants to go, he may 'put the brakes on', leading him to brace his feet wide to slow you down.

Fig. 31   Ko-uchi-gari

Fig. 32   Ko-uchi-gari

Grip

Take the standard grip on the sleeve with the left hand, and hold at about collar-bone height with your right hand.

Footwork

The footwork for this throw is very simple. Adjust your position slightly so as to move right side on to the opponent. From this position, lunge forward with your right foot, through the legs, then bring the sole of your right foot sharply back against the back heel of the opponent's right foot, sweeping it abruptly *forward* (Fig. 32). The direction in which you hook this foot is important. As with O-uchi-gari, do not lift the leg up, or kick it to the side, but make sure that it is brought forward in the direction that the toes are pointing. Also make sure that you do not hook the opponent's right foot into your left leg. If you started the throw from the slightly right side on position, this will have taken your left leg out of the way.

Armwork

The sudden hooking or sweeping action of your right leg must combine with a sudden pushing action of both hands. In fact, the more sudden these two movements are the better, since the opponent may stiffen his whole body in a sort of shock reaction. This would make the throw much easier to bring off.

Push the opponent obliquely down with both hands, aiming the knuckles at a spot about four to five feet behind him. As you are knocking away his right leg, it helps to push his weight slightly over on to that leg. This would change the direction that you throw him in slightly, making it more to his right-back-corner than straight back.

Finish

As the arm and leg actions combine, throw your bodyweight into the opponent, and follow him down as he falls to the mat. Drive your hands towards the mat, but do not crash on top of your partner. As the opponent topples backwards he may start to swing round to your left; if he does so, turn with him and go down, but still keep him 'on the hook', that is, your right leg hooking strongly and the arms pushing down.

Tsuri-komi-ashi (propping drawing ankle)

There are two versions of this throw. In one, the opponent's ankle is blocked (sasae-tsuri-komi-ashi) and in the other, it is swept back (harai-tsuri-komi-ashi). The former is described here.

To picture the action of this throw, imagine a door (unhinged) which you are supporting. The side facing you is bare wood – the other side is painted. Your aim is to drop the painted side of the door on the floor over towards where you are standing. This is done by first balancing it on the bottom right corner, then pivoting the whole thing round, letting it drop to the floor roughly over the spot where you were standing. Of course, you must move aside as you make the pivoting action and let it drop.

An opponent standing square on to you can be likened to a door, especially if he is stiff. The throw often succeeds when you can make the attack very suddenly, shocking the opponent into a stiff reaction. Against a floppy, relaxed person it does not work so well.

Opportunity

The throw can be done against an advancing right ankle, an ankle level with the other one, or on a retreating one. The method described here is against an ankle level with the other one, in other words, against a square on stance. Action can be taken when the feet are still, or when the ankle you are about to attack is level with the other one as it moves forward. This is a very neat and workable opportunity.

Grip

Take a very secure grip with your left hand on the opponent's right sleeve near the elbow. Hold his lapel with your right hand, about own shoulder-height.

Footwork

Step forward and slightly out to the right with your right foot, twisting your foot so that it points at the opponent's right foot. Transfer your weight to the right foot and lift up your left leg, stretching it out so that the sole of the foot is placed directly on the front of the opponent's right ankle (Fig. 33). Bear in mind that the opponent is thrown forwards. If you do not move out to the side at the start of the throw, you will be in the way.

Fig. 33   Tsuri-komi-ashi   Fig. 34   Tsuri-komi-ashi

Armwork
The action of the left arm is extremely important in this throw. As your feet move into position, pull the opponent strongly forward with your left arm over your blocking left foot, then as he starts to trip over it, twist your body round to the left and aim the pull at your left hip. The right arm assists the action of the left. First pull the opponent forward then as he starts to trip over your left foot, push him down.

Finish
The whole action of the throw can be seen as a large twisting one. The opponent is literally twisted off his feet (Fig. 34). Right from the start of the throw, twist the body strongly round to the left, particularly the head and shoulder, co-ordinating this with the pulling action of the left arm and the blocking left foot.

An old piece of advice with this throw was to achieve 'stomach contact'. This indicated the necessity of moving the whole body in close to the opponent, particularly the stomach, not allowing a large gap to appear between the two. A common fault is for the thrower to bend in the middle, pulling his backside back.

A certain amount of nerve is sometimes necessary to finish off the throw. At the end of it there comes a stage where the thrower feels he is going to fall over backwards with the opponent landing on top of him. At this point he must not let go and panic, but must hang on even as he is falling backwards and twist violently round, making sure that it is the opponent who hits the mat first.

Hiza-guruma (knee wheel)

This throw is similar to the previous throw, Tsuri-komi-ashi, except that the thrower's left leg blocks the opponent's knee and not the ankle. However, the inclusion of the word 'guruma' in the name indicates the different emphasis in the throwing action. When the ankle is attacked in Tsuri-komi-ashi, there is a large element of 'trip' in the throw, but with the blocking attack to the knee in Hiza-guruma it is most unlikely that the opponent will *trip* over. Thus it is not the block at the knee which is crucial to the success of the throw, but the action of the thrower's body, which in this case is that of 'guruma' or spin/twist.

Once in position for this throw against a static opponent, there is almost no leverage to push or force it through. It is most effective when the opponent helps with the action, which is to say when he reacts into it. If a reaction can be created and used, this throw can be successfully brought off.

Grip
Take a strong hold with the left hand on the opponent's sleeve by the elbow. With the right hand take hold of the lapel at own shoulder height. Both men stand in the right natural stance.

Reaction
Step back strongly and to the right with your right foot and pull violently with your right arm. This is to give the impression that an attack is going to take place to that side. With practice a mere twitch of the right hand may be sufficient. Sensing a throw to this side, the opponent may throw his weight the other way, that is, over his right leg and knee. Do not wait for this reaction, since to wait would be too late, but lift your left leg up placing the sole of the foot against the opponent's right knee. Your left leg should be fairly straight which means that your initial step back with the right foot should have been quite a

large step. Having faked first to the right to get a reaction, the arms now reinforce the reaction by jerking strongly over the left. This should completely unbalance the opponent, bringing all his weight over on to his right leg (Fig. 35).

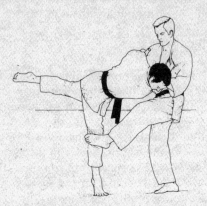

Fig. 35   Hiza-guruma

Finish

As your left leg blocks and your arms pull the opponent over the block to his right-front-corner, twist strongly round to your left and flip the opponent off his feet, pulling vigorously all the while with your left arm in a curve down to your left hip.

With this throw it is essential to get the feel of using your own bodyweight. The action is similar to that of throwing the hammer. Once you have got the reaction, lean back and swing the opponent off his feet. The whole 'wheeling' action is a large one, not a tight little flip.

Hang on tight to the bitter end of the throw, making sure that it is the opponent who hits the mat first.

Ko-soto-gari   (minor outer reaping)

Quite often this throw is confused with the advancing-foot-sweep (De-ashi-harai), especially when it is done on its own and not as the second string to a combination attack. The difference lies in the directions in which the opponent is thrown. The De-ashi-barai throws the man down to his side whereas Ko-soto-gari throws him backwards.

Opportunity

The usual opportunity for this throw occurs when the opponent steps forward with his right foot, not so much directly towards you, but diagonally forward to your right side. The throw can be done as he steps, or after he has stepped forward.

Grip

Hold at about opponent's collar-bone height with your right hand and gather a lot of cloth with the left hand just above his elbow, that is over his triceps muscle.

Footwork

The opponent has his right foot back but is about to step forward with it. The thrower parallels this position with his left foot forward and right foot back. As the opponent steps forward, step back with your *right* foot (not, as usual, with the left), swinging it round slightly behind your left foot.

Armwork

As you step back with your right foot, pull strongly with your left hand so as to make the opponent step diagonally forward and inside your left foot. If you think of pulling the opponent's elbow towards your right hip bone, this will have the right effect. As your left hand pulls towards your hip, push the opponent's weight back and over his right heel (to his right-back-corner) with your right arm.

Finish

Having coaxed the opponent's right foot into the desired position, continue the left arm pull down towards your right hip, and the push with the right arm. If the armwork has been successful, the opponent should be balancing almost entirely on his right heel. To finish the throw, bring the sole of your left foot to the back of his right heel and scoop it across towards your right foot (Fig. 36). This will send the opponent crashing to the mat. The scooping action of the left foot and the action of the arms must combine.

Okuri-ashi-barai (side-foot-sweep)

There are two main foot sweeps. There is the advancing-foot-sweep (De-ashi-harai) which is done against a single foot as it steps forward, and there is the side-foot-sweep, which is done against both feet as the

Fig. 36   Ko-soto-gari

opponent skips sideways. The latter is the one which scores most and will
be described here.

General fighting movement around the mat is usually directly forward
and back or obliquely forward and back, interspersed with circling or
turning movements. The footwork for this is of the usual walking variety,
that is right foot forward (or back), followed by left foot forward (or back),
and so on. However, quite often the two fighters will skip or move directly
sideways without crossing their feet (inside ankle bone moves towards
other inside ankle bone). This movement creates a good opportunity for
the throw.

These sideways skipping movements are fairly frequent but may not
last more than two or three steps. The thrower must be ready for these
very brief opportunities. This throw relies almost entirely on timing, with
little or no power required at all.

Opportunity
The opponent skips sideways to his right. If he is moving reasonably
fast he will in fact bounce along and at the split second his feet move
close together he will often be completely clear of the mat. This is the
moment that both feet must be swept away since there will be almost no
resistance.

Footwork
As the opponent skips sideways, synchronise your movements with his

and skip along at the same rate. The split second that the opponent's legs are at the widest, start to sweep the opponent's *trailing* left ankle in towards his leading right ankle (Fig. 37) with the undersole of your right foot. It is important to understand that the opponent's legs are swept away from behind as he moves along, not blocked.

Fig. 37 Okuri-ashi-harai   Fig. 38 Okuri-ashi-harai

When making the sweep, stretch your right leg out as far as possible (think of making it a long range throw) and try to skim the little toe edge of your right foot along the mat as far as you can. It is not a scooping action but a sweeping action along the mat, as if you were brushing away some dust. Make the sweep bold and vigorous, right through to the other side of the opponent's feet, and this will send him crashing to the mat (Fig. 38).

When practising this throw, make three skips sideways and sweep on the last one. Since synchronisation of footwork is all important, you can practise the three-step movement and then just gently unbalance your partner on the last step with your right foot. It is not necessary to throw every time. Once you have got used to the three-step timing, practise the throw with two steps and then just one.

For best results try to control the opponent's arm on the trailing side of the body. If you have taken a standard right hand hold but are sweeping with your right foot, transfer your right hand hold from lapel to opponent's left sleeve.

Although the arms have a minor part to play at the end of the sweep, in pulling the opponent down to the mat, it is generally better to forget about their action, since thought in this area often detracts from making a really full-blooded sweep. Concentrate on producing a whip-lash of a foot-sweep.

Kata-guruma   (shoulder wheel)

This is very much a strong man's throw, since the thrower has to lift his opponent up bodily off the mat. The knack here is to get into the lifting position fast. Once this is achieved there is little that an opponent can do to stop the lift, short of having a low ceiling which he can push down from, unless he is actually too heavy for the lifter to handle.

Grip

Take a standard grip with right hand on the lapel about own shoulder-height and left hand on the sleeve. In the Nage no Kata* the left hand grip for this throw is shown, not on the outside of the sleeve at the elbow, but on the inside, by the crook of the arm. Take whichever sleeve grip feels comfortable.

Armwork

Pull strongly with your left arm forward and up so as to lift the opponent's right arm forward and away from his body. Jump into a squatting position close to the opponent's feet and duck your head under his right arm-pit. At the same time, drop your right arm through the opponent's legs and clasp his right thigh with your whole arm.

Finish

Continue the strong pull of the left arm so that the opponent is pulled forward off-balance, over on to your shoulders. For maximum leverage in the position try to put your head not so much directly under his arm-pit but lower down the rib cage nearer his centre of gravity.

Once you have swung the opponent on to your shoulders, straighten the legs and lift him up off the mat (Fig. 39). To unload him off your back, continue the pull with the left arm and swing him off your left shoulder, not directly forward over your head. The opponent is lifted

*(see Chapter 13)

on to the right shoulder, wheeled (hence the name) across the back, and dropped off the left shoulder. The jump into position, pull on the back and lift, should be done as explosively as possible.

It is possible to make the throw to the other side with a slight adjustment of grip. Hold a little higher with the right hand, then duck your head under his left arm-pit and grasp his left thigh with your left arm, duplicating all the moves as above but the opposite way.

The faster Kata-guruma is done, the less lift is needed to wheel the opponent over.

Fig. 39   Kata-guruma

Tomoe-nage   (stomach throw)

This is one of the self-sacrifice or Sutemi-waza throws. It involves dropping to the mat in order to throw. The key element in this and the other sacrifice throws is the destructive effect on the opponent's balance of the thrower's weight suddenly falling to the mat.

Opportunity
Tomoe-nage is often done against a stiff opponent, who is bending forward somewhat, pushing his opponent away with rigid arms. It can be done successfully against a considerably larger or taller man. Although

the throw can be brought off against a static opponent, it is often most effectively applied against a man who is stumbling forward, almost off-balance. This may come about, for example, when he makes an attack with one of the rear leg throws such as Ko–uchi–gari or O–uchi–gari, but misses and stumbles forward.

Grip
Take a left hand grip on the end of the opponent's right sleeve and a right hand grip on the lapel about own shoulder-height. The thrower can hold both of the opponent's sleeves if he wishes.

Footwork
Step forward with your left foot, sit down close to your opponent's feet. Place your right foot on the opponent's stomach at about belt level (Fig. 40).

Fig. 40   Tomoe-nage   Fig. 41   Tomoe-nage

Finish
The above three movements must be done virtually simultaneously. If done so the opponent will be swung up into the air on the end of your right leg (Fig. 41). When you have got him in the air, swing him over your head or left shoulder, pull your hands in towards your body, and drop him on his back on the other side of your body. The pulling

action of the hands is to turn the opponent in the air to ensure that he will land on his back.

To ensure that the opponent does not get off the hook, make sure that he is thrown over your head or left shoulder. If you should throw him over your right shoulder he has the opportunity to put his left arm to the ground and escape the full throw. The opponent can be thrown more directly to the side with this throw, in which case, the rule is: throw him over the side on which you hold his sleeve.

There are two common faults. One is to let go with the hands as the opponent is two-thirds through the throw. This often fails to turn him completely over on to his back. The grip with the hands must be maintained until after he has hit the mat. It might be necessary to continue into groundwork. The second fault is to make the leg in the stomach too relaxed, in which case the leg crumples and the opponent collapses on to the thrower.

For real success with this throw, a certain amount of courage is required. Success depends on a lightning-like drop to the mat, but the throw is often done timidly for fear of thumping the back. This must be completely disregarded. The more fully committed the thrower is, the less likely it is that there will be any discomfort. The thrower hangs on to the opponent when he drops, which helps to break the fall.

Uki-waza (floating throw)

The mechanics of the throw are simple, but the opportunity is crucial to success. The word 'floating' does not describe the mechanics of the throw except in so far as it applies to a type of movement done by the opponent. Uki-waza is done when the opponent 'floats'. This means the sort of movement produced when resistance is suddenly taken away. For example, if one was using one's shoulder to push open a door wedged firmly shut and then it suddenly gave way, then one would go 'flying' or 'floating' through the doorway. This sort of uncontrolled movement often comes about in Judo after a fierce attack by one party against a man who either moves slightly out of the way of the direct path of the attack or who rides with it. This throw can be done nicely following a lunging Ko-uchi-gari.

Grip
The grip is standard – left hand on the sleeve with right hand on the lapel.

Opportunity

Get the opponent to lunge forward with a Ko–uchi–gari attack. As he comes in for the throw, jump back from it with both feet, encouraging him to stagger forward. Having jumped back immediately drop to the mat under his feet and stretch out the left leg, bringing your thigh into contact with his right ankle. Your right leg stretches the other way.

Armwork

As the opponent staggers forward and you drop down under his feet, pull him strongly forward with your left arm over your outstretched left leg, then down to your left hip. As he goes flying over your leg (Fig. 42) and his shoulder nears the mat, jerk sharply up from your left hip with your left hand to make sure that he lands on his back (and not the point of his shoulder).

Fig. 42   Uki-waza

For maximum success with this throw the thrower must drop like a dead weight.

Yoko-gake   (side dash)

This is very much like Tsuri-komi-ashi but it is done with a sacrifice throwing action. Done correctly it can be a very heavy throw for the opponent.

Grip

An unusual grip is shown, but this is the one recommended by the late Kyuzo Mifune (10th Dan) who specialised in this sort of throw.

Start by taking the standard grip – left hand on sleeve, right hand on the lapel. Then shift the right hand to hold over the opponent's left arm, taking the cloth by his elbow.

Footwork

Drop back to the floor and place your *right* foot on the opponent's left front ankle, pushing it back as you drop to the floor. At the same time pull strongly forward with your right arm (Fig. 43).

Fig. 43 Yoko-gake

The sudden effect of the thrower falling to the floor and the driving action against the opponent's left ankle will drop and twist him to the mat. Make sure that the opponent does not land on top of you but to your right side.

For good results with this throw, a reaction similar to that used for Hiza-guruma should be obtained. After taking the grip, twitch to your left side (as if going to make a right side throw) and then when he reacts the other way, twist strongly to your right and drop in for the throw.

A modern analysis of throws

The traditional classification of Judo throws is in terms of which part of the body plays the leading role. For example, there are arm-throws where the action of the arms is said to be especially important, but it is difficult to say that the actions of the other parts of the body are un-important. Leg-throws do not work if the arm action is wrong.

When one attempts to analyse Judo in more definite terms one soon comes up against the daunting complexity of it. At the end of the day it might be easier to learn the Gokyo of forty throws than bend one's mind around a thick tome of modern scientific description.

In Judo there is really only one sort of throw and that is where the man lands on his back. However, there are different paths he can take to get there and the thrower can help him there in different ways.

When a thrower makes a move there are perhaps three main ways of doing it. He can turn around and throw (e.g. shoulder-throw), he can move straight at his opponent (Osoto-gari) or he can fall down and throw (Tomoe-nage etc.). The person being thrown, can either go straight backwards (O-uchi-gari) or if he is to go in any other direction, such as front or side, he must be turned so as to land on the back. If he is turned there are two main ways. First, he may be rotated forwards (like a somersault) or he may be rotated sideways (twisted off his feet). Furthermore, rotation may not be the main feature of a throw, but lift. A man may be lifted up (Kata-guruma) although at the finish of the throw he must be turned to land on his back. A thrower can push or pull his opponent off his feet or spin him off his feet, and can do it by exerting force against one or more parts of the body. Whatever forces and positions are required for a throw done on a static opponent, they may be modified if he is moving.

Thus a throw can be looked upon as an amalgam of interdepending conditions which all change if one changes.

In practice the various types of positions and forces merge into one another. A throw is only rarely a pure forward rotation throw, for example. Thus a Seoi-nage may be a mixture of lift, forward and side rotation. What tends to change any throw is that the opponent is trying to stop whatever you are doing and an expert Judoman adapts to the situation.

However, there are certain generalisations that can be made about the most common types of throw and which, if understood, will help you to make quicker progress.

Weak and strong directions of posture

Make the following experiment. Get somebody to stand with their feet about shoulder-width apart. Instruct them to resist your push without moving their feet. First try pushing him from one side to the other. It will be seen that he can brace his legs against this sideways push and that a lot of energy is required to unbalance him. This is his strong direction of posture.

Next place a hand on his chest and push him backwards (or pull forwards). With almost no effort at all on your part, he will topple backwards (or forwards). This is his weak direction of posture. Thus it is much easier to throw a person directly forwards or backwards than it is sideways. Fig. 44 illustrates this principle.

However, most people in Judo stand with one foot and side forwards, and this changes their weak/strong directions. In all cases the new

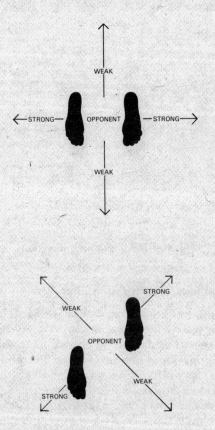

Fig. 44   DIA. Weak/strong directions

directions can be worked out by taking a line between the two big toes, then taking a ninety degree line through the centre of it.

A person can be thrown along his strong direction if he is moving in that direction sufficiently fast or if you can make him react strongly into it.

In many throws one of the opponent's legs are attacked (Harai-goshi, O-uchi-gari). When this is a part of the throw, it is usual to get as much of the opponent's weight on the attacked leg as possible. This then means that the throw is not necessarily along the weak direction, but more to the corners of the stance, such as right-front-corner (see Fig. 45).

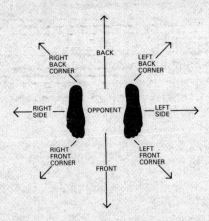

Fig. 45   DIA. Throwing directions

Breaking of balance and throwing directions

There is a stage in any throw when 'contact' is made. This may be when the attacker's leg touches the opponent's leg in the leg-throws (ashi-waza) or when body contact is made in the hip-throws (koshi-waza). At this contact point, for the throw to be most successful, the opponent should be off-balance. This will be his point of minimum physical resistance. A human body is like a tall narrow box. If you wanted to push such a box over, a push aimed a few inches from the top of the box would be enough to start it falling over. However, if you start to push a body, it will start to fall, then quickly regain balance by taking a step forward or back. Total destruction of the balance can be achieved by making the push or pull very suddenly or by making the push or pull and blocking the balance-regaining step at the same time.

Unbalancing a person is not a preliminary to a throw; it is part of the whole thing and is usually done by the arms as the feet and body move into position. Not only is it more difficult to throw a person who is on-balance, but there is a much greater risk of being counter-thrown.

Fig. 45 illustrates the names of the directions in which the balance is broken, and the directions in which the body is thrown. Not only is a person's balance broken in a particular direction but he is usually thrown in that direction too. With any throw know the direction in which the opponent is to be thrown, and keep your effort true to this line. If a throw is along a person's weak direction, but half-way through the throw it veers into his strong direction, he of course will be in a much better position to stop it. Also when attacking to the corners of an opponent's stance, when you have pushed the opponent's weight over on to a leg you want to attack, care must be taken that no weakening of the pull or unbalancing to that corner takes place, since this will give the opponent the chance to shift his weight to his other foot (and escape from the throw).

When an opponent is unbalanced to a corner, the push or pull that is required to do this must be very strong, since it is usually one arm that does most of the work, (especially for the turn-around throws such as Harai-goshi).

Centre of gravity

In some of the forward body-throws, such as Seoinage, the opponent is somersaulted (rotated) forward and dropped on his back. To rotate a body forward successfully, a block, such as one of the thrower's hips or one of his legs, needs to be placed on or just below the opponent's centre of gravity over which the body can be push-pulled. The centre of gravity is usually about the level of the belt. When coming in for such throws, aim to get your own belt level with or just below the opponent's belt. Experimentation with body position will show which is the best one with which to smoothly and easily turn the opponent forward.

Advice often given in Judo is 'come in low'. This refers to coming in beneath the centre of gravity. Since the opponent's defensive action is often to lower the centre of his gravity, by bending the legs and sinking the hips down, it is often necessary to anticipate this and come in even lower. When this happens the action is usually completed by first lifting the opponent up (by straightening the legs) then rotating him to the mat. This is the extra lift that is often needed with forward twist and somersault throws. A very fast Judoman would not need to put any lift in to his forward somersault throws, since if he got into position fast enough he could rotate the opponent before he could drop lower. However, it is good policy to build 'lift' into this sort of throw, first, because there is no guarantee that you will make contact with the opponent before he can lower his centre of gravity, and secondly because the human body is virtually powerless once it is in the air.

Even a body moving forward quite fast will not necessarily rotate round any block that might be put in front of its centre of gravity, since the opponent's hold on the thrower enables him to push or pull himself lower. Most Judomen, however, move at a speed at which they feel they have control. 'Get him up' and 'come in low' is sound Judo advice. Avoid the 'flop-and-drop' style of Judo.

Getting in low is sometimes interpreted to mean coming in so low that the thrower's hips are about level with the opponent's knee caps. The effect of this action when it can be done, is to trip rather than rotate the opponent, and if it is done very suddenly it can be very successful. For most purposes, however, it is only necessary to position oneself just below the centre of gravity.

Depth of entry

With the turn-around throws the thrower turns around and moves in towards the opponent. However, depending upon how the opponent is moving, the extent that the thrower has to move in towards the other man varies. If the opponent is more or less standing still, the thrower cannot move in right close to his man since he would then have no room to unbalance him. In this case he should move in half-way and pull the opponent the other half towards him. In other words 'body-contact' should take place at a point half-way between the two bodies. If the opponent is moving forward reasonably fast the thrower can pivot on the spot and throw, since the opponent should be moving on to his body.

By moving in too close to the opponent, throwers often get in the way of their own throw. When meeting half-way a strong action with the arms is essential. The vigorous use of the arms at the beginning of all throwing techniques cannot be over-estimated. The arms should never be mere linking chains between the two bodies.

If your opponent is moving backwards, it must be remembered that he is moving out of any backwards throw you have in mind. The faster he moves the more difficult it becomes, unless the thrower can stay close to the opponent. This would mean lunging into the throw at the same speed with which the opponent is moving backwards. The more slowly the opponent moves backwards the more chance there is for a backwards sweep or topple throw.

When the opponent circulates round the thrower, the opportunity is given to twist him off his feet or sweep his feet away sideways. The twisting action can be done from the centre of the circle (by moving in closer to the opponent), or from the perimeter of the circle (with a sort of hammer-throw action).

Simultaneous opposite forces

In many throws the opponent is moved with two opposite forces. In the backwards leg-throws, for example, the legs are hooked forward as the upper body is pushed backwards. In the forward body-throws, especially the ones that use one leg to balance on, and the other to assist (Uchi-mata, Harai-goshi), the leg sweeps back as the arms pull forward. It is essential to work the two forces *simultaneously* on the opponent. If there is a slight gap between the two, the opponent can often slip off the throw. However, when the thrower is perhaps not fast enough and the opponent stiffens in anticipation of the throw, a deliberate gap between the actions will often succeed. In this case it is surprise rather than mechanics that works.

See-saw

With many of the top-scoring throws such as Uchi-mata and Osoto-gari, the action of the thrower's whole body is very much like that of a see-saw. The supporting leg of the thrower is like the base of the see-saw with the upper body and lifting leg forming the see-saw platform. As one end moves up, so the other end goes down. In Uchi-mata, for example, the thrower's head swings down towards the mat as the leg sweeps up. If the head does not swing down, the leg cannot swing up. See Fig. 46 for illustration of this action.

This see-saw action can be practised quite easily against the wall of the Dojo. Rest one arm on the wall and practise swinging the leg up and the head down. The tendency is for beginners to try to keep their heads up when making a throw. It takes a little courage to drop one's head down to the mat in this throwing action. It is important not to let your nerve fail right at the end of such actions, releasing the grip, and putting the hands down to the mat to save yourself. Hang on tightly to your partner, have faith in the throw, commit your weight into it and all will be well – you will not hurt yourself.

Use of the head

The head is a heavy part of the body and can be used to assist in most throwing actions. With the backwards throws, the head is thrown forcefully into the direction of the throw right from the start. In the forward

Fig. 46   DIA. See-saw

rotation and twist throws the action of the head is often delayed. Usually the head stays looking forward, perhaps at the opponent's face, and then a split second after the body has twisted into position, the head is whipped round into the direction of the throw to add extra impetus to the twist.

Head and hands

In many of the turn-around throws (Seoinage, Tai-otoshi) it is essential to keep the hands and head near each other for the main part of the throwing action. The tendency when turning around is for the hands to drift a long way away from the head, or vice versa, and this indicates loss of efficiency in the arms. This often happens when the opponent braces back against the forward pull but it must not be allowed to happen. As you start to turn around, the hands should be pulling the opponent forward; as you go fully into the turn the hands should still be close to the shoulders and only start to move away after the main part of the throw when the opponent is dropping down to the mat.

Timing and power

It is useful to distinguish between those throws which require a lot of timing and those into which one can put a lot of power. With the former, such as Okuri-ashi-harai, timing is all essential. If the timing is out, the throw fails miserably. With the other type such as Osoto-gari, it is possible to be slightly out with the timing, but still be in a position to 'power them through'.

If one is tending to specialise in a 'timing' throw it is well to be quite candid about one's physical abilities. Great speed and accuracy are necessary and without these you may be wasting your time.

The throws that tend to succeed are those in which the thrower is able to exert his force directly against the opponent. For example, in Uchi-mata (p. 30) the feature of the action is that the thrower is able to lift his opponent directly up off the mat with his right leg. The same goes for Seoinage; once in position the thrower is in an extremely strong lifting position. In Osoto-gari (p. 22) the thrower does not have the advantage of lift, but he has strong leverage and can exert his strength to the maximum through the action of his right arm and right leg.

With other throws, however, there is much more reliance on weight to make the throw succeed. For example, the falling-down (Sutemi-waza) throws depend on the thrower suddenly abandoning his balance and hurling himself to the mat, the action of which catapults the other man off his feet.

The timing throws depend on neither leverage, lift, nor weight but on very fast movement and accurate positioning at the exact moment the opponent is at his weakest.

Of course any throw must be done as fast as possible. It does not mean that because Osoto-gari is a power throw that it can be done slowly or without correct timing. All these factors must combine for a perfect throw.

Three-phase throwing actions

Most complete throwing actions can be analysed into two stages. The traditional classification is:

1. Tsukuri
2. Kake

In *Judo Kyohon*, the only book ever written by Kano, he says,

'Tsukuri is when you break the opponent's balance and move your body into position, and Kake is when you do the technique. When doing Randori, especially throws, at first, emphasis is placed on the practice of Tsukuri, and then later, on Kake. The reason for this is, if the Tsukuri is good but the Kake is weak the technique can be brought off, but if Tsukuri is incomplete, the strong opponent will stop the throw and in the case of a weaker opponent there is the danger of causing injuries to him.'

Although Kano only broke a throwing action down into two phases – Tsukuri and Kake – the first phase (Tsukuri) is in two parts. Breaking the balance is the first (Kuzushi) and moving the body into position is the second and most Japanese experts talk of the Kuzushi – Tsukuri – Kake progression. Of course a throw does not consist of these three *separate* phases. They all blur into each other and are inter-dependent.

A more modern three-phase analysis of movement in sport is that of Minel. He says there is:

1. the preparatory phase
2. the main phase
3. the recovery phase

Characteristic of the preparatory stage is a small movement in the opposite direction to the main movement. This is often seen in Judo and is frequently a give-away sign as to the real intention of the thrower. The breaking of balance action would also probably belong to this phase. The 'main phase' is probably equivalent to the second stage of Tsukuri (moving the body into position) and Kake (finishing the throw off). The 'recovery phase' marks the return to balance and original position. Sometimes in Judo there is no return to balance since both thrower and thrown crash to the mat, but it has always been regarded as good Judo when the thrower maintains his balance.

One could probably add another stage to all the above classifications. Very often a throw is the result of subtle manoeuvrings by the thrower. The opponent is induced into a chain of movements, the last of which puts him in a bad position (but good for the thrower). Most experts have these patterns of movement which they try to draw their opponent into. Quite often these are rhythmical in nature, and a clash between two good men can be seen as an attempt by one to impose his rhythmn on the other.

Thus a throw may be the result of:

1. general manoeuvring around the mat
2. small movement into the opposite direction of main action
3. breaking of the opponent's balance
4. moving the body into position
5. a heave to the mat
6. recovery of balance and position.

The 'right throw' for you

There are a variety of reasons why people adopt one throw rather than another. The throw that people tend to concentrate on is often the first throw that felt comfortable to do and which had some success. It is frequently the first throw that is taught to them. In all cases the throw chosen might not be the best throw. Success in the early stages with a throw does not mean necessarily success in the later stages. One good guide with throws is to see where they place in the contest-statistics. If your main throw is low on the list it may well mean that you will have problems throwing good men with it. Of course any throw done unexpectedly with the speed of lightning may throw the Olympic champion, but it is as well to recognise that the odds are against this.

In the first place it is often the physique that determines your throw, but if you develop it with proper training then you broaden your potential to do other throws. Never reject a throw because it does not feel right for you. The reason might simply be because your legs are not strong enough. If you regard Judo as a method of physical training (which it is meant to be) you will obviously want to develop an all-round physique and this would mean doing such things as Kata and gymnastics (see the chapter on off-mat training). This training in turn will broaden your repertoire.

A good throw

To score an Ippon, a person must be landed more or less squarely on his back with impetus. In addition, a 'good' throw has the following qualities.

First, a good throw is a *compact* throw. The opponent should be dropped to the mat by the most direct route possible, either in a tight roll or twist forward or with a sharp drop backwards. Second, it should be *sudden* to the extent that the opponent may not even know what throw it was that took him over. Third, it should be *comfortable* for the thrower.

4

Counter-Throws

There are four actions that can be taken against somebody who tries to throw you.

1. block the throw
2. move out of the way
3. counter-throw
4. counter-attack.

A counter-throw (Kaeshi-waza) is a throw *appropriate* to the movement and position of an opponent who is moving in to throw you. A counter-attack is *any* throw fired off against an opponent who is either moving in for a throw or who has moved out after a failed throw. A counter-attack can be very successful but depends on the nerve and speed of the thrower. Of the first three responses, the counter-throw is the most positive. It may score, but even if it fails the opponent may be deterred from attacking again. In free-fighting these four actions need to be varied, since an element of unpredictability in your responses is the safest course.

A counter-throw which is fired off as an almost unthinking response to an attack probably stands the best chance of succeeding. A person who waits for his opponent to attack in order to make his counter-throw, or who deliberately invites a throw by putting himself in a bad position, requires great subtlety. It is usually very obvious when a person wants to make a counter-throw – quite often he will change his grip in preparation for it. A further consideration is that the IJF rules penalise a person for passivity. An attack is expected at frequent intervals, which leaves little scope for the deliberate counter-thrower.

Nevertheless, a badly done throw often gives the opportunity for a counter-throw, and every Judoka should be able to take the opportunity when offered.

Most throws can be countered. Some counter-throws have names, many do not. The *types* of counter-throw are few in number and can be summarised as follows:

1. pick-up
2. fall-down
3. leg sweep
4. side-step

One of each of these types will be illustrated.

Pick-up   (Te-guruma)

This move can be made against most attacks when the attacker moves in close. It is usually done against the forward body throws such as Harai-goshi, but it is also possible to do it against a leg-throw attack such as O–uchi-gari.

Fig. 47   Te-guruma

Fig. 48   Te-guruma

As the attacker moves in for, say, Harai-goshi, drop your centre of gravity by spreading and bending your legs, insert your left arm through the attacker's legs and, grasping the top of the nearest thigh (which should be the attacker's right one in a right handed attack), lift him bodily off the mat by straightening your legs (Fig. 47). To make this lift, it is essential not to lose your balance from the initial attack, and to lift with a straight back. When gripping the thigh, use your whole arm and pull the thigh into tight contact with your body.

To finish off the throw, pull the attacker face-down to the mat with your right hand. Half-way down he will twist of his own accord and land on his back (Fig 48). Once you have got him up in the air it may be necessary to push your stomach forward so as to swing his legs clear of yours.

Fall-down (sutemi)

This type of counter-throw is made by dropping to the mat, using a Sutemi-waza type of technique.

As the attacker moves in for, say, Ippon Seoinage, drop your left hand and wrap it round the opponent's waist, catching him before he can make the full turn-in for the throw. Continue the throw by dropping down to the mat in *front* of the attacker in a downward spiralling action, driving

Fig. 49   Yoko-guruma

Fig. 50   Ura-nage

your right leg between his legs (Fig. 49). As you spiral down to the mat hold tightly with your left hand and spin the opponent over your body to hit the mat.

It is important to show that you have avoided or stopped the action of the first Ippon Seoinage, otherwise in contest a referee might feel that it was the first attack that dropped you to the mat, and give the points to the other man. This counter is called Yoko-guruma (side-wheel).

Against a similar sort of attack another Sutemi-waza counter can be made, called Uranage. It is a very spectacular and heavy counter.

As the opponent moves in for his attack, drop your left arm as before and catch the opponent around the waist just before he has time to make the full turn.

Finish the throw by picking the opponent up and arching backwards, head diving towards the mat (Fig. 50). To make sure of a score, twist to the left just before you hit the mat so as to drop the opponent on his back first.

Fig. 51   Counter to O-uchi-gari

Fig. 52   Counter to Ko-uchi-gari

Leg-sweep

Against most leg attacks (such as O-uchi-gari and Osoto-gari) a counter throw can be made by sweeping away the attacking leg or the attacker's supporting leg. For example, when the opponent makes a right-sided attack with O-uchi-gari, step back a little way with your right foot, and as his right leg is about to hook away your left leg, sweep it across to your right side with your left leg (Fig. 51). Continue the action by swinging the opponent's body backwards and over to your left, using a strong action of your arms and shoulders.

Against a right-sided Ko-uchi-gari attack, lift your attacked right foot and block the opponent's supporting left ankle (Fig. 52) and twist him over to your right in a Tsuri-komi-ashi type action. This has to be done very precisely but when brought off can be a very spectacular counter.

With all the leg-sweep counters, maximum results are obtained when the opponent makes a *strong* leg attack. If he throws his weight into the attack you will be able to counter him quite effortlessly.

This point has to be borne in mind when learning these moves. If your partner does not attack hard, the counter will seem clumsy and unworkable.

Fig. 53   Sukashi to Uchi-mata

Fig. 54   Sukashi to Uchi-mata

Side-step   (sukashi)

Against some throws, if you simply step out of the way, the attacker will virtually throw himself with little or no assistance from you. It is possible to score this way, though the referee would have to see that you deliberately stepped out of the way.

A spectacular example of this type of counter is the counter to

Uchi-mata. Against the Uchi-mata attack, simply move your left foot behind your right foot and twist your body round a little to your left.

As the Uchi-mata man moves in for the throw he will expect to make lifting contact with his right leg between your two legs, but if you have taken your left leg out of the way his right leg will go sailing past (Fig. 53). If he has made a really full-blooded attack he should throw himself from the force of the throw; however, he can be helped over with a twisting action of your arms. The counter can also be re-inforced by bringing your left leg across (after his right leg has gone sailing past) and making ankle to ankle contact with a Tai-otoshi like movement (Fig. 54) and completing as for Tai-otoshi.

5

Combination Throws

Although theoretically a man with only one very good throw could win the world championships, in practice it never works out this way. Sometimes one meets a person with a physique which virtually cancels out one's throw: for example, a shoulder throw expert meeting a very short and squat opponent. Or, for example in a championship, other competitors, having seen you do Uchi-mata, may stop the throw by keeping their legs very close together when it is their turn to fight you. Something extra is always needed, whether it be another throw or just a feint as a lead-in to your main throw. These extra moves can be combined in a number of ways. They are:

1. a feint into a throw
2. a throw into a throw and
3. a throw and a throw.

Feint into a throw

In this combination of moves, the thrower pretends to make an attack with one throw, then, as the opponent reacts against the threat, he proceeds instantly to his main throw which seeks to utilise to maximum advantage the opponent's reaction. The reaction may be to move, stiffen or relax, all of which can be used.

It is essential to make the initial feint a real threat. A weak feint will create no reaction and may invite a counter throw. A certain amount of judgement, which only practice can give, is required here. If the first move is made too forcefully, the thrower may lose balance or expend most of his energy, and in both cases he will not be able to make the main attack.

It is necessary to understand what a feint-throw combination involves. When it is the *intention* to throw with the second move, the opponent must be deceived and the thrower must divide his energies. The feint must be sufficiently deceptive, it must be recognised, and it must be reacted to. The problem here is that good men are difficult to deceive and that beginners may not recognise the feint (especially when it is done very quickly). Perhaps this sort of combination works best on nervous twitchy people.

One frequently sees apparently successful combinations of this kind but they are often unintentional: the thrower makes a determined attack with one throw, gets stopped and then moves on to another appropriate move and scores. In this case the second scoring move was not planned in advance.

A typical feint-throw combination is from Ko-uchi-gari (Fig. 32, p. 45) into Seoinage (Fig. 13, p. 28).

Attack with a fairly determined Ko-uchi-gari. The opponent will often react to this by stepping back with his attacked right leg. As he does so, instantly drop your right foot to the mat, close to the opponent, swing the left leg round and back to the left and move the arms into position for Seoinage. This also works well in reverse. A feint for Seoinage will often cause the opponent to brace back, spreading his legs wider than usual, and this will give the opportunity to continue with Ko-uchi-gari.

A reaction to any attack is nearly always in the opposite direction. If you try to throw somebody forwards he will brace backwards and vice versa. Most combinations work on the front-back directions mainly because this is the postural line of weakness (see p. 60). Other possibilities are switching from right to left side and vice versa, and half opposites, i.e. front to left/right. There are also limited opportunities for combining moves both in the same direction.

Theoretically most front and back throws should be capable of combination but some work more easily than others. Typical combinations are:

Ko-uchi-gari	→	Seoinage	→ Ko-uchi-gari
O-uchi-gari	→	Tai-otoshi	→ O-uchi-gari
Hiza-guruma	→	Osoto-gari	
Uchi-mata	→	Ko-soto-gari	

Throw to throw

The difference between this sequence and the previous feint-throw one is that in the first there was only one real throw, preceded by a feint diversion. In this sequence a real attack follows a real attack.

With the feint-throw sequence the reactions between front and back were mainly exploited but this may prove very difficult with a throw-to-throw combination. With a really determined leg-throw to the rear, for example O-uchi-gari, the chances are that if he has really thrown himself into the attack the attacker will hardly be in a position to suddenly switch direction and go the other way. Most probably he will be staggering in the direction he wants to make the throw. However, this indicates how two throws can be put together and that is with both working in the same direction. In actual practice the opportunities are limited.

Fig. 55   Nidan Ko-soto-gari   Fig. 56   Nidan Ko-soto-gari

If you try to throw somebody forward, they will stop the attempt by bracing and sinking a little. If you then try to make another throw forward, the initial resistance will still stop you. If there is some movement forward it may be possible to combine say Harai-goshi and a *low* Seoinage. In this case it is the switch in levels which may catch the opponent by surprise.

It is with throws to the rear that combinations are more likely. The chances are with rear throws that the opponent will simply move off them and continue moving backwards. This then gives you an opportunity for a second attack.

A typical sequence is from Osoto-gari to Nidan (two-step) Ko-soto-gari. When you attack with Osoto-gari it is often the case that the opponent stops the throw and you are locked in position with your right leg hooked around his right leg. When this happens, push into the opponent so as to get him moving backwards and place your *right* foot on the floor (Fig. 55). Keep him moving backwards, transfer your weight to your right leg, then swing your left leg round and sweep away the opponent's left leg (Fig. 56). The whole action is a continuous move in the same direction.

Another combination of throws both in the same direction is Ko-uchi-gari into O-uchi-gari and vice versa.

Throw and a throw

With the previous methods of combination, the thrower moves *in* for an attack/feint then moves on (from the close position) to the next attack. With this method of combination the attacker moves in for one throw and (if it fails) then moves *out* at arm's length and attacks with another throw. What the attacker tries to do here is to exploit the fear and anticipation of the first throw. For example, a fierce attack with a shoulder-throw (a forward-throw) will put the opponent on the alert for another such attack. It may be that he will physically react against it by hanging back, or he may mentally react against it by merely watching out for it. To take advantage of this, the attacker could make a rear throw attempt, such as Ko-uchi-gari. When such an attack is completely unexpected it can succeed brilliantly. The first attack must be very strong (not just a feint) and the opponent must genuinely fear or anticipate another similar attack. The second attack (in the opposite direction) does not have to follow immediately after the first. Provided that the fear or anticipation of the attack is there, the second throw can follow minutes later.

The second throw may not score, and then ensues a battle of wits with the thrower trying to catch his opponent out with a wrongly anticipated throw. If we call the first throw A and the second B, then the thrower would seek to put them together in some pattern of attacks such as A-A-B! or A-B-A-B-B! or any sequence which catches the opponent on the hop.

As with previous combinations, this pattern of attacks usually exploits the front to back (and vice versa) throwing directions or possibly right to left side throws. There is limited opportunity for a right- and left-side combination, since it is usually necessary to change grips for a throw on the other side, and this invariably gives the game away. There are just a few throws that can be done to the left with a right-side grip, such as Tsuri-komi-goshi (see Fig. 26, p. 39).

An A–B combination could be further enhanced with a third attack, which should be as different as possible from the first two. It could be a left-sided throw following a right-sided front and back combination, or it could be a drop-down (Sutemi-waza) throw. The more unpredictable you can make your attacks the better.

Whichever way you combine your throws, it is absolutely essential to be able to do each throw independently. When you can make a good Tai-otoshi and a good O-uchi-gari, then you can start to combine in feint-throw, throw to throw and pattern attacks. One throw can be slightly weaker than the other but it should always be a threat.

Another approach that some high-ranking Japanese masters insist on is to master one throw so that it can be done from almost any grip, against any opponent and in any situation.

Combination Judo, or reaction Judo, as it is sometimes called, is not necessarily a higher or more advanced type of Judo. A man who could do say two or three throws well could become the Olympic champion without necessarily using his throws in combination. They can be used individually purely in response to the situation. A time and motion study of a series of championships in Japan up to national level showed that solitary attacks far out-numbered combination throws to a ratio of 10 to 1.

6

Hold-Downs

Free-fighting Judo is generally divided into two activities. Most of the time the contestants try to throw each other, and this is called standing-work or Tachi-waza; but it often happens that the fighters fall to the ground, where the fight may continue, in which case it is called ground-work or Ne-waza. On the ground the fighters try to gain a submission (from an arm-lock or strangle), or try to hold the opponent on his back for thirty seconds. Arm-locks and strangles can be done standing, though they are rarely seen. In World championship competition, groundwork accounts for about twenty-five per cent of all scores and this is roughly the proportion of time spent on the ground in relation to standing work.

The hold-downs, or pins as they are often called, are the main method of scoring on the ground. Of the twenty-five per cent of scores that groundwork as a whole took, hold-downs scored twenty per cent, and armlocks and strangles together only accounted for five per cent.

However, the rules limit the opportunities for winning on the ground, and if these were changed there might be a much higher incidence of groundwork scores.

People who take up Judo for self-defence sometimes criticise hold-downs as being valueless. Historically, they were methods of capturing the enemy. Once knocked down, he was held and then either trussed up or immobilised until help arrived. In practice, however, a skilful groundwork man might use a hold-down to momentarily subdue his opponent before moving on to an arm-lock or strangle.

Although there are many hold-downs, there are only a few basic ones and most of the rest are variations on these. Six holds will be described here. For a hold-down to score, the opponent must be held down largely on his back. There is not a strict definition of a hold-down and it is often left to the discretion of the referee. The referee tends to call 'Osaekomi!' (holding!) when he sees a recognised hold-down, which is usually one with a Japanese name.

Kesa-gatame   (scarf hold)

Sit beside your opponent in the space by his right arm-pit. Leaning across his upper body, wrap your right arm around his neck and hold tightly. Gather up his right arm with your left arm and tuck it under your left arm-pit, trapping the wrist between your upper arm and body. Gather the jacket at the elbow with your left hand and hold tightly. Having secured the opponent's arm and head, spread your legs (Fig. 57).

Fig. 57   Kesa-gatame

In this hold three basic points have to be maintained. They are: pressure on the opponent's rib cage with the weight of your upper body, a tight hold round the neck and a complete securing of his right arm. The securing of the arm is probably the most important point. The legs are spread wide to prevent any forward or backward push by the man underneath.

When the opponent starts to struggle in this hold-down it is essential to maintain the same relative positions of the two bodies. If the man underneath tries to move away in anti-clockwise direction, or in closer in a clockwise direction, the man on top must move likewise, maintaining the same pressure on the ribs all the time.

Kamishiho-gatame   (upper four quarters)

This hold-down, and especially its many variations e.g. Kuzure-kamishiho-gatame, is very popular in competition. Like any other hold, some time is required to get the feel of it. It is like riding a horse. The mechanics of sitting on the animal are simple, but learning to stay there when it moves takes some time.

Kneel by your opponent's head, with the knees spread wide and the opponent's head directly between. Keep your body as low and as flat as possible and slide both of your arms along the mat, *under* the opponent's shoulders, to grasp his belt on both sides. Tighten the hold by pulling the opponent's belt strongly up towards his rib cage and wedging your elbows tight into the body. Bear down with as much weight as possible on the opponent's upper body. Your face should rest near the solar plexus (Fig. 58).

Fig. 58   Kami-shiho-gatame

Once the opponent moves in his attempts to escape, it may be necessary to stretch out one or both legs to brace oneself. As he tries to turn off his back, one or other of his shoulders will start to rise and the man on top must then shift his bodyweight slightly so as to bear down on that shoulder.

Yokoshiho-gatame   (side four quarters)

Kneel alongside the body of your supine opponent, with both knees spread wide and touching the body. Take your left arm round and under his head, and catch the collar on the far side. Thread your right arm down through his thighs, under the left thigh and catch his belt firmly on the other side (Fig. 59). To tighten the hold, bear down with the weight of your upper body, lock your arms tight and look at your opponent.

Fig. 59   Yoko-shiho-gatame

As he starts to struggle it may be necessary to stretch out one or both legs and lower the stomach to the floor. The opponent may also try to sit up, in which case be ready to bear down with your bodyweight on his chest.

Tateshiho-gatame   (lengthwise four quarters)

With the previous holds, the attacker's weight has been mainly off the opponent, lying to one side or end of his body. When the holder stiffens his grip it is most difficult for the man underneath to move him; like trying to lift a long piece of wood from one end.

In this hold, however, the holder has most of his weight on top of the opponent and he maintains the hold by restricting the movement of the opponent's arms and legs. As before, the basic version of the hold is shown here, but a person wishing to improve his hold-down ability would have to learn all the variations, regarding each as having the same holding potential.

Lie on top of your opponent, stomach to stomach, and hook both feet under his buttocks. Take your left arm over and then under the opponent's left shoulder and clasp his belt under the side of his body. Stretch the opponent's left arm out above his head and pass your right arm underneath it and clasp your own right lapel at about chest height. Trap the outstretched arm between the right side of your head and right shoulder. Hold the outstretched arm tightly and bear down with your full bodyweight on it. Lock the legs tightly around the opponent's hips (Fig. 60).

This is an awkward hold to learn. At first it feels uncomfortable and the man underneath can easily roll you off, but with practice the feel for it can be acquired, and eventually stronger and bigger men can be held.

Fig. 60   Tate-shiho-gatame

Ushiro-kesa-gatame (reverse scarf hold)

In this hold-down the attacker's position is almost exactly the same as in Kesa-gatame, except that he is facing the other way; in other words he will be looking at his opponent's feet rather than his head. This hold is often done as a continuation from a failed Kamishiho-gatame, although the attacker can move straight into it as the opportunity occurs.

Kneeling by the opponent's head and left shoulder, slide your right arm under the opponent's right shoulder and arm and grasp his belt. Sit down in the gap between the opponent's left ear and shoulder, pick up his left arm, tuck the wrist under your left arm pit and hold his elbow with your left hand. Stretch the right leg forward so as to almost run along the left side of the opponent's body and stretch your left leg back in the opposite direction (Fig. 61).

Fig. 61   Ushiro-kesa-gatame

When settling in for the hold, push tightly into the space between the opponent's left ear and shoulder, lean against the side of his head, and push your stomach into his left arm. Pull strongly on his belt with your right hand and tuck the right elbow firmly under his right shoulder. Do not give the opponent any slack in which to move his upper body. A variation with the right arm hold is to take it over the top of the opponent's right arm, catch the belt as before, but firmly press the right elbow into his arm-pit. A hold very similar to this can be taken as a follow up to an arm-roll to the side (see Fig. 87, p. 117).

Kata-gatame   (shoulder holding)

This hold is most often taken as a continuation from Kesa-gatame, when the man underneath has freed his right arm in an attempt to break the hold-down.

Quite often a man trapped in Kesa-gatame (see Fig. 57, p. 83) will try to free his right arm; when this happens he will often use it to try to push the man holding him backwards, pushing against his head or under his chin. When this happens, use your left hand to push his right arm down across his face. Swiftly bring your head down to the mat, trapping the right arm between your head and the opponent's head. Clench both of your hands together, locking the opponent's right arm firmly between the two heads. To complete the hold-down, move from the sitting position into a kneeling one, with your right knee close to the opponent's body and your left leg stretched out to the side (Fig. 62). Do not allow the man underneath any freedom of movement of his head or right upper arm. Sometimes the hold around the opponent's neck is so tight that he will submit to the choking pressure.

Fig. 62   Kata-gatame

Hints on holding

Strength has to be built into a hold-down. It is not something that works magically if you are in the right position. The sort of strength required is isometric strength or static strength. One famous groundwork man used to train by walking up steps carrying a box loaded with bricks in front of him. Eventually his arms and shoulders became so strong in that carrying position that when he locked into a hold-down (with a similar arm position such as Kamishiho-gatame) very few men could escape.

Quite often the man who succeeds with a hold-down is the one who is thinking of gaining a groundwork advantage even while he is crashing to the mat with his opponent from standing-work. Having gravity on your side is a distinct advantage, so as you are falling, or the moment you hit the mat, twist into the upper position, squashing him with your weight. Avoid landing underneath him. Keep your weight on the opponent while you decide which hold-down you can settle into. Which hold-down you take is mostly determined by the position you fall into in relation to your opponent. If you are by his head, then Kamishiho-gatame is indicated, and so on.

Do not hang on to holds till the bitter end. If the man underneath is breaking free or perhaps rolling you off, it is essential to stay on top. Thus when the hold is slipping, switch to something else or simply let go, but make sure that you have still got the advantage of gravity.

Under the rules it is possible to switch from one hold-down to another without interrupting the thirty second count. However, only do this when necessary. There are no extra points for switching, and there is a big risk that the hold-down as a whole will be lost.

The 'make or break' time for a hold is the first few seconds, during which the man underneath will expend most of his energy in two or three frantic bursts to get free. Hang on grimly for this period and settle in deeper during the brief periods of rest.

7

Arm-Locks

To win with an arm-lock it is necessary to cause pain to the elbow joint, forcing the opponent to submit. The man who submits does this by tapping twice, either on the opponent or on the mat. If his arms happen to be trapped he can use his feet or, failing this, shout out 'Maitta' (I submit).

Pain is caused to the elbow joint by either straightening the arm further than it should go or, when it is bent in a figure L-shape, rotating the forearm one way or the other to the limits of its natural rotation and a little beyond.

Although there are only three basic methods of moving the arm, the various positions and situations in which the three can be done are endless.

The time to attack the arm is when the opponent has carelessly extended it. Since he can pull it back to safety very sharply, the attack must be quick and smooth. This must be done to a point just short of causing pain; then the last move is done carefully and more slowly so as to avoid injury.

Juji-gatame (cross arm-lock)

In recent years this arm-lock has been very prominent in international competition. This is probably because of the entry of the Soviet Union in world Judo. Soviet Judomen were largely pulled from the ranks of their Sambo wrestlers who specialise in this type of arm-lock. It can be done from several positions, of which two will be described here.

After falling from a throw such as Tai-otoshi, a man will often land with his right arm extended. This is because the thrower in a right-sided attack would be holding the right sleeve with his left hand. Taking instant advantage of this, move your right foot close in to the opponent's body, swing your left foot over his head and place it down by his left ear. At the same time, drop to the mat, sitting as close as possible to the opponent's right shoulder and catch his outstretched arm between your legs.

Keeping the arm firmly trapped between the legs, lie back, catching hold of his wrist with your right hand, and pull the whole arm down towards your stomach and chest (Fig. 63).

Fig. 63   Ju-ji-gatame

Depending upon how stiff the opponent's elbow is, the pain may come on as his arm nears your chest or it may be necessary to increase the leverage by lifting your hips up off the floor and continuing the pull towards your chest.

Make sure that you are sitting away from the opponent's body at a ninety degree angle, close to his shoulder, and that the white underside of his arm is pointing directly upwards.

Variation on Juji-gatame
The aim in Juji-gatame is to trap the opponent's arm between your legs. This variation illustrates how it can be done when the attacker is lying

on his back with the opponent kneeling between the legs (a common groundwork situation).

Grasp the tip of the opponent's right sleeve with your left hand. Roll on to your right hip and swing your left leg right round over the opponent's right shoulder and down in front of his face. Keep the arm held tight and straight between your legs.

In this situation there are three possibilities for gaining the submission:

1.   apply immediate pressure against the arm, using your own arms and legs and straightening the body (Fig. 64)

2.   capsize the opponent over to your left, using your left leg to push in that direction, then making the normal juji-gatame movements against the arm as in Fig. 63,

3.   roll over on to your stomach, bringing the opponent down on to his face, then pulling his arm up against your body to gain the submission (Fig. 65).

Fig. 65   Ju-ji-gatame stomach down

Fig. 64   Ju-ji-gatame from underneath

In this third move, the opponent, sensing the danger to his arm, may roll head over heels forwards, in which case the attacker follows the movement by twisting on to his right side, then stomach, then on to his back, maintaining a tight hold of the opponent's arm all the way. This move will have brought both men back to the basic Juji-gatame position as in Fig. 63, and pressure is applied by lifting the hips and pulling the arm in to the body.

Ude-garami (entangled arm-lock)

This is the arm-lock applied to the arm when it is in a bent L-shaped position. As with Juji-gatame, it can be done in a variety of positions. Both fighters have collapsed to the mat in the course of standing work. One lies on top of the other in almost a Yokoshiho-gatame position. We will assume that the man underneath has left his left arm lying bent on the mat.

Quickly grip the opponent's left wrist with your left hand, holding in such a way that if you extended your thumb it would point to the opponent's elbow. Next pass your right hand under the upper part of the opponent's left arm and grasp your own left wrist with your knuckles pointing upwards (Fig. 66).

To apply pressure to the elbow joint, lift up your right shoulder and right side of the body, so as to look at the opponent's feet, maintaining all the while the entangled arm position. Very little movement of the body is required to put pressure on the elbow, so care must be exercised.

Once you have learned how to make the correct arm positions against the bent arm lying conveniently on the mat, practise it from the Kesa-gatame sitting position, catching the left arm as it comes up to push you away. As you catch the arm and push it back down towards the mat, roll on to your stomach and make the arm moves as before. It is important not to fumble the grips. Practise this move till you can slide quickly and smoothly into position. It will not take many repetitions before you can automatically take the right grips.

Variation on Ude-garami

In this variation of Ude-garami the arm is rotated the opposite way to that previously described. There are several opportunities for applying this lock, but probably the most common one is when the opponent is kneeling between the legs.

Lie on your back with the opponent caught between your two legs. With your left hand grip the opponent's right wrist. Next take your right arm over the top of the opponent's left elbow and down to grasp your own left wrist. As you take this grip bend the opponent's arm into the L-shape figure. Having trapped the arm, move to your left about six inches and roll on to your right hip. Pull the opponent face down to the mat and, maintaining the entangled grip, lever his right forearm upwards to bring pressure on the elbow joint (Fig. 67). Care must be taken that the shoulder joint is not attacked. This means levering *only* the forearm up and not the whole arm.

Fig. 66   Ude-garami

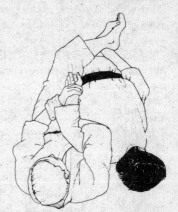

Fig. 67   Ude-garami from
between legs

Waki-gatame   (arm-pit lock)

This is another arm-lock applied on a straight arm. The leverage this time is under the attacker's arm-pit. One way that this lock is applied is against an opponent on all fours.

Kneel beside your opponent, resting your weight on his back. The first move is to break the opponent down so that he collapses on his face and stomach. To do this, insert your right knee between the opponent's left knee and elbow, then, using your right knee, knock away his elbow. Remember that the man underneath is balanced between two knees and two elbows, and the combination of having your weight on top of him, and having one of his supports knocked away, is sufficient to flatten him (Fig. 68).

Having flattened your opponent, quickly grasp his left arm by the wrist with your two hands, and pull his arm under your right arm-pit.

Fig. 68   Waki-gatame   Fig. 69   Waki-gatame

As you do this, swing into a sitting position, resting your back on his back.

To bring pressure on the elbow joint, push down with your arm-pit on the upper part of the opponent's arm and lever his forearm up in the opposite direction (Fig. 69).

Care must be taken not to lift the whole arm upwards, since this will bring pressure on the shoulder joint which is against the rules. When the pressure is correctly applied the opponent's arm barely moves.

This arm-lock can often be made on an opponent who is rolling off his back on to his stomach. When he rolls in towards you he will often lead with one arm. (Try rolling off your back on to your stomach and notice how one arm is flung over the body.) If you are sitting or kneeling beside your opponent when he does this, catch that arm, swing it under your arm-pit, roll him flat on to his face and apply the pressure as before.

Ude-gatame   (arm-press)

This is another of the arm-locks done on a straight arm. It is mainly taken from a loose Kesa-gatame position before you have had time to catch the opponent's head and arm, and when he carelessly reaches up to your collar.

Sit beside your opponent in the Kesa-gatame position. Often in this position the man underneath will reach up with his left arm to catch your lapel by your right ear. When he does this, cup both hands and place them one on top of the other round his elbow, and, with a shrugging action of the right shoulder, trap as best you can his wrist between your head and shoulder.

The pressure is put on the elbow by pulling the joint in towards your chest and rotating it in an anti-clockwise direction. At this point the opponent's head and shoulders may rise off the mat to alleviate the pain on the elbow. If he does this, swing your left leg over his head and hold it in position (Fig. 70).

Fig. 70   Ude-gatame

This lock can also be done as you kneel beside your opponent. As he reaches up with his left arm as above, catch his arm in the same way and pull his body close in to your knees. For greater leverage stand on your right foot and rest your right shin and knee on his body.

General hints on arm-locks

Arm-locks are not difficult to do and do not require much practice to learn compared with throws. Some of the grips are complicated and it is necessary to practise them so that the lock can be taken smoothly and quickly. It is fatal to hesitate half-way through a move since the opponent can very quickly snatch his arm back to safety. Once you have learned the basic methods of making the lock against a straight or bent arm, applying them in other groundwork situations becomes easier and easier. You only have to become aware of arms to see countless other opportunities for making a lock.

Juji-gatame and its many variations is especially popular in competition and nobody who wants to specialise in arm-locks can afford to neglect it.

Arm-locks can be done when standing and can be very effective not only for scoring purposes but for breaking up a stiff, defensive pair of arms. However, it is not possible to apply an arm-lock as you fall to the mat – that is against the rules. The opponent may drop to the mat in an attempt to escape the pain of the lock, and you may follow him down to finish it off. The lock must begin to take effect in a standing position before transition to the ground can take place.

8

Strangles

Judo is one of the few combat forms which allows strangles. The distinction is sometimes made between a strangle, which cuts off the blood to the head, and a choke which shuts off the air to the lungs, although in practice both actions are mixed. For scoring purposes no distinction is made. Care must be taken, however, that the vertebrae in the neck are not twisted or stretched in any way, as this would constitute a neck-lock which is forbidden and very dangerous.

The aim of a strangle is to make the opponent submit. A submission is indicated by two sharp taps of the hand, either on the mat, or on any part of the attacker's body.

There is no clear definition of a strangle in the rules, which sometimes leads to confusion among beginners. Most attacks to the neck use the jacket, while there are one or two which are done 'bare', in other words with the arms directly on the neck. The classic film strangle, using the fingers of both hands to squeeze into the neck, is not allowed.

To gain maximum effect from any strangle, the hands have to be positioned very precisely and quickly. If the hand hold is an inch out of position the attack will fail. When practising these techniques, experiment with the position of the hands until you get it just right.

The other general rule about strangles is to back up the action of your arms with the strength of your legs. Often the power of the arms alone is not sufficient to strangle somebody who is wildly thrashing around. The legs are used to wrap around the opponent's body so as to hold him in position while the strangle is applied.

Okuri-eri-jime   (sliding collar-lock)

This attack is often made against an opponent who is on all fours on the mat. Move in from the opponent's left side, slide your left hand under his chin to grasp his collar just under his right ear. At the same time throw your right leg over the opponent's back to sit astride him, as if riding a horse, with the feet not touching the mat but thrust back through the thighs (Fig. 71). Continue the movement by throwing your weight over to the opponent's right side, capsizing him with your body-weight and the firm grip of your legs. As you fall to the side, snake your right hand under the opponent's right arm-pit to grasp his left lapel at about chest height.

Fig. 71   Okuri-eri-jime

Once on the ground, maintain a strong controlling grip with your legs, and pull with your left arm strongly into the opponent's neck (Fig. 72). It is absolutely essential that the collar grip with your left hand be as deep as possible, with the thumb inside the jacket and positioned right under the right ear, or even further round the neck. Note that the strangling arm goes *over* the shoulder while the controlling arm (in this case the right one) goes *under* the arm-pit. Provided the left hand is deep enough, a submission will be quickly gained.

Fig. 72   Okuri-eri-jime

Juji-jime   (cross strangle)

This is a strangle done facing the opponent. It often happens that, having fallen to the mat on his back, with the opponent half kneeling beside him, the man underneath will quickly move against a threatened hold-down. A common defensive move in this case is to swing one leg over and catch the man on top between the two legs. As a general rule, this should be the only time in groundwork that you lie on your back (apart from being held down). With the other man caught between your legs you are in a strong attacking and defensive position, and the man between your legs is not regarded as holding you down.

The strangle is straightforward. Cross your forearms, palms uppermost, and insert your hands deep into the opponent's collars, grasping the lapels with the fingers inside, just under the ears. To force the submission, pull the opponent's head down towards your chest and pull both elbows out away from your body (Fig. 73).

Fig. 73   Ju-ji-jime

In practice, the arms are not crossed before insertion into the collar, as this tends to give the game away. Insert one of your arms in deep, then quickly follow up with the other one. The more deeply one hand is inserted into the collar the less deep the other has to be.

Take care that the legs play an active part in the attack. Keep them wrapped around the opponent's trunk and cross them at the ankles. Hold the opponent firmly with your legs, but on no account squeeze the trunk, as this will be regarded as a kidney squeeze (do-jime) which is strictly forbidden.

Hadaka-jime (naked strangle)

This move would probably be regarded as a choke since it is applied more directly against the windpipe than the other strangles in this chapter. It is called 'naked' strangle since it is done with the bare arms, without using the jacket for leverage.

Fig. 74 Hadaka-jime

Fig. 75 Hadaka-jime

Clasp your two hands together – right hand on top, back of the hand facing up, left hand underneath, back of the hand facing down. Kneel behind your opponent and, using the bony edge of the forearm above the thumb, pull it into his throat, causing him to submit.

In Fig. 74, Hadaka-jime is shown against a sitting opponent for clarity of illustration, but in practice it is almost never done this way.

In practice, this choke is often applied against a man who has been flattened face-down into the mat. Sit astride your face-down opponent, reach behind and lift up both of his legs by the trousers and slide both of your feet in underneath his thighs. Then leaning forward, proceed with the choke as above. When the opponent resists the choke, push both hands down and round his neck, making a fist if necessary, but do not decide in advance which forearm is going to actually apply pressure on the throat. Usually the opponent will resist more strongly on one side of his neck than the other, and when you feel this, the appropriate fist can penetrate right round the neck on the weak side. When applying the pressure in this situation bear down on the back of the opponent's head with your chest (Fig. 75) and pull your forearm in towards your chest.

Care must be taken when pushing your hand round the neck. It must go under the line of the jaw. It is against the rules to touch the face, and the bony edge of the jaw marks the limits. Properly done, this can be a most uncomfortable and effective choke.

Kata-hajime   (single wing choke)

This choke is applied from behind, and is extremely powerful once the attacker is in position. As with all such moves it is essential to move the hands into position at maximum speed. It can be taken from a variety of positions; here it is described against a man lying on his left side, his back towards his attacker.

Kneeling behind your opponent, slide your left hand under the head, round his neck, and grip his upper right lapel at about collar-bone level. Next, insert your right hand between the opponent's body and right arm, close to the elbow. With your right forearm inserted in the crook of the elbow, lift the arm up away from the body, then drive your right hand down behind the opponent's head, sliding your right forearm over your left (the forearm must not be grasped).

Pressure is applied by pulling back strongly with your left hand and pushing down past the opponent's head with your right forearm (Fig. 76). With correct hand and arm positioning, this choke fits neatly into place and causes instant and unbreakable pressure against the neck.

If the opponent tries to roll away from you, wrap both legs round him from behind and continue the choking action as before, going with his roll.

Sankaku-jime   (triangular strangle)

This is a very powerful strangle that can be applied with the legs. Under the rules it is not permitted to squeeze the opponent's neck or head between two legs, but it is allowed if an arm is trapped with the head. People with short thick legs may find this difficult to do and others may have to experiment with the leg positions before they can find the correct comfortable position. It can be done against opponents in a variety of positions; the most common one is described here.

Fig. 76   Kata-hajime

When lying on the ground with the opponent caught between your two legs, he will often try to break through the legs to attempt a hold-down. Frequently the opponent will insert one arm between one of your legs and his body and try to lift it over his head. It is this move which gives a good chance for Sankaku-jime.

When the opponent starts to get past your legs as above, you must first give him the impression that you are resisting his attempt to lift your leg. Let him slowly lift it, then as it gets near his head, suddenly release the resistance and swiftly place your leg along the back of his neck and shoulders (not down his back), tucking the crook of your knee (the right knee, if it is the right leg that the opponent tried to lift) against the side of the opponent's neck. Instantly bring up your left leg and place the back of the knee over the top of your right foot. This is the crucial part of the strangle. Your right foot must fit snugly behind your left knee, not just the big toe but the whole foot up to the ankle. This will give an unbreakable hold round the opponent's neck and arm (Fig. 77).

Fig. 77   Sankaku-jime

From the start of the move the attacker must hold the sleeve tip of the opponent's right arm with his left hand and, as the legs swing into position, the right arm must be pulled forward and straightened. This will make it easier to pin that arm against the head, making the unit around which the legs have to be wrapped that much smaller.

To apply the pressure, pull your left foot down and tighten both thighs. Sometimes the strangle may not be immediate, but it is worth staying in position since the effects often build up slowly.

There is a danger that the opponent may try to stand up and lift you off the mat, in which case the Referee must call 'Matte' (break!). To prevent this, it is advisable to try to topple the opponent sideways once you have got the legs in position.

Usually an arm-lock can be applied against the arm that is trapped with the neck in a move similar to Juji-gatame.

Hineri-jime   (twisting strangle)

This strangle does not strictly have a name, but it is sometimes referred to by high-grade Japanese teachers as Hineri-jime or twisting strangle.

This strangle is unusual since, at the start of it, the arms do not affect the opponent's neck, but the attacker can scissor the neck between his fore-arms by twisting his body. Sometimes, if the opponent twists, he can put the strangle on himself. Since there is no direct threat at the start of the strangle it is often fairly easy to put the hands into position. It can be done from a variety of positions but here it is shown as an attack from underneath.

Lie on your back with the opponent caught between your legs. Reach up with your right hand and catch hold of the opponent's collar (by his left ear) with your fingers on the inside of the jacket and thumb on the outside. Reach up with the left hand and hold the opponent's collar by his right ear, this time with the thumb inside the collar and the fingers outside (Fig. 78). The arms do not cross as in Juji-jime.

Fig. 78   Hineri-jime

Fig. 79   Hineri-jime

The man between the legs will naturally try to cross your legs to attempt a hold-down. In this case offer him little resistance and allow him to cross over your right thigh. As he crosses over your thigh and moves round to your right side, roll on to your left shoulder and scissor your two forearms together, bringing the right one under the left and up under the opponent's chin (Fig. 79). This arm action is very much like that in Morote-seoinage.

To apply pressure, drive your left forearm up into the opponent's throat and pull down with your left hand. Take care to keep your hands near your shoulders.

Sometimes from this position the opponent on top will dive over the attacker in his attempt to escape the strangle and will reverse the positions. Nevertheless, the strangle can be pursued in this reversed position.

As the man dives over the top, take care to keep your forearms crossed and locked into position and roll with him. As he lies underneath, rest your right shoulder on his chest and continue the arm action as before.

As with all strangles, success is dependent upon how exact the grip on the lapel is. In this strangle, the hands should almost be touching each other round the back of the opponent's neck. If you imagine the grip that would be taken on a vertical rope if you wanted to climb it and then moved your hands into a horizontal position, that is the grip that is required on the opponent's collar.

In practice it is better to take the right hand grip first, then, as the opponent moves over your thigh, quickly take the left hand grip. This would help to deceive your opponent as to your real intentions.

9

Escapes from Hold-Downs

Not every Judoka likes doing groundwork. There have been noted champions whose groundwork was weak, as well as those who used their skill on the ground to great advantage. Although the rules favour the standing fighter, it is unwise to neglect this branch of Judo, since good groundwork opportunities often present themselves.

In competition, hold-downs take most of the scores on the ground, with arm-locks and strangles some way behind. This suggests that it is wise to concentrate on hold-downs, while it also follows that the ability to escape from hold-downs would be a valuable asset. The groundwork specialist must study all groundwork moves, but the Judoka who has no particular interest in groundwork could work on escapes alone in order to keep out of trouble.

Escapes from hold-downs are not like magical tricks that provide the key to open the locked door. A man who clamps a hold-down on is difficult to dislodge; however, there are certain weaknesses in every hold-down and, of course, the man on top may make a mistake. With every hold-down there are perhaps three or four possible ways to escape and it is necessary to work between them all. In general terms the hold-down is at its weakest during the first ten seconds or so. It is a very good policy to 'go berserk' as soon as the hold-down is put on. This is when you will be at your strongest and when the holder will be most unsettled. Often frenzied activity here will completely shatter the hold.

There are four ways of breaking free from any hold-down. The first is the technical break. This is the break that exploits the rules. For example, in a contest, if a hold-down is taken close to the edge of the contest area, in the course of the struggles both men may move completely out of the contest area. At this point the referee will break the hold-down and call both men back to the middle to recommence fighting in the standing position. In club training, of course, this does not strictly apply, but it is wise to look at one's position and direct one's struggles so that movement out of the training area may take place. With technical escapes of this kind, it is necessary to be conversant with the current contest rules as these change from time to time.

A second way to avoid a hold-down is to apply a strangle or an arm-lock on the person holding you down. There are a number of ways of doing strangles in particular from underneath but there is a large element of risk in doing this. The vital seconds are ticking away while you are trying to catch your attacker. Even though you may have the strangle strongly applied, the man on top can often just prolong his resistance the extra ten seconds or so to give him the hold-down score.

Actual escapes from holds are of two varieties. The first is the 'roll-over' where the man on top is simply rolled off with the man underneath taking the upper position. In the other kind of escape, the man underneath wriggles out from the hold, perhaps turning on to his stomach, and the man on top stays where he is but loses the hold-down.

There is one other method of escaping from a hold-down which should perhaps be regarded as a technical break. This is when the person underneath manages to trap one of the legs of the person on top between his two legs. Although from an unknowledgeable spectator's point of view, there is no change of position and the man on top still looks in command, the hold-down is broken and the referee will call it as such. When trapping the leg you must trap it between your two legs and cross them. It is not enough to just pinch it between your feet.

The tendency for inexperienced people caught in hold-downs is to try to bodily heave off the man on top, rather than try to wriggle out. This simply wastes a lot of energy. The golden rule when wriggling out is to discover precisely what is stopping you, then go round it or break through it. Once one point is broken, the entire hold-down usually crumbles.

Even when heaving (rolling-over) the opponent off there are specific techniques that require much less strength and energy than the undirected heave.

Escapes from the four main hold-downs will be illustrated using some of the methods above.

Escape from Kesa-gatame

This escape is not strictly a 'roll-over', but involves a sudden change of position with the man underneath swinging into the upper position. This is a popular way of escaping from Kesa-gatame.

Balance is important in groundwork and in this hold-down the man on top maintains his balance by leaning on your ribs. If you remove this support it is easy to unbalance him backwards and reverse the positions.

The first move is to catch your opponent's jacket with your right hand which will be trapped under his left arm-pit. This will give you some leverage when pushing him backwards. Next, lift both of your legs up in the air, keeping them together and straight, and swing them away from the holder, down towards the mat (Fig. 80). The reason for swinging the legs in this way is to achieve a sort of rocking-horse effect. As you swing your legs down, lock your stomach, and this will swing your upper body up. As the legs go down, also shift your body away from the holder's body. This will remove his support on your rib-cage. Continue the whole rocking-horse action and push your opponent backwards and down with your right hand as you swing up into a sitting position (Fig. 81).

Fig. 80   Escape from Kesa-gatame

Fig. 81   Escape from Kesa-gatame

Once you have achieved the sitting position, clamp a hold-down on, but take care not to get pushed backwards yourself.

Escape from Kamishiho-gatame

In this escape the man underneath seeks to break one part of the hold-down and wriggle on to his stomach. The idea is not to move the man on top out of the way. For a hold-down to be valid, the person held must be more or less on his back. If he can wriggle on to one side or on to his stomach, the hold-down is 'broken'. The referee's command and signal for this is 'Toketa!' accompanied by a waving of his hand.

When this hold-down is fully established, the person on top seeks to immobilise the opponent's shoulders and upper arms. When this happens, the man underneath cannot roll from side to side and of course he cannot sit up, since the opponent's body is bearing down over his face.

The first move in this escape is to free one of your shoulders and arms. Lift both of your legs up in the air, keeping them straight and together as in the previous escape. Swing them down sideways, locking the stomach muscles and use the downwards impetus of the legs to twist on to your right shoulder. This rocking-horse movement, this time sideways, is a very important groundwork move. If you do not lock your stomach muscles tight, your legs will merely hit the mat and your upper body will stay where it is. However, if you can learn to maintain the tension in your mid-section, you will be able to lift or twist your upper body even with considerable weight on it.

Having twisted on to your right shoulder you should find a slight gap between your opponent's right upper arm and your right shoulder. Thread your right arm through this gap and catch hold of the opponent's trousers at his right knee. Using this for leverage, twist on to your stomach (Fig. 82). By threading your arm through the gap you will have unlocked one of the key points in the hold-down and there will be little to stop you turning off your back.

Fig. 82   Escape from Kami-shiho-gatame

Having turned off your back do not feel in any great hurry to do anything. The hold-down is broken and you are not required to make any other move. You may, of course, want to continue the fight on the ground, but if you do not, clamp your elbows in tightly to your side, protect your neck, stay stomach down, and wait for the referee to stand you both up.

Escape from Yokoshiho-gatame

This move illustrates the roll-over variety of escape. It is difficult to move a body completely off you, especially when that body is firmly clamped into position exploiting your weaknesses. However, like everything in Judo, there is a hard way and an easy way to do things. In this case it is the direction in which you try to roll the man off, that is important.

To start the escape, use your left hand to catch the opponent's belt at the back and pull it up strongly towards his head using your left elbow to pin his head down to the mat.

The opponent is now ready to be rolled off. To start the action, bring your right foot up close to your right buttock, placing it on the mat. Next bridge on to your left shoulder, pushing strongly off your right foot. Keep the opponent's head clamped down with your left arm and roll him over your left shoulder and over his own left shoulder, bridging strongly throughout the whole move (Fig. 83). The opponent can also be helped over by using your right hand to push his legs over.

Fig. 83   Escape from Yoko-shiho-gatame

It is important to roll the opponent diagonally over his left shoulder and not simply straight forwards in a head over heels movement. The direction over his left shoulder is the weak one.

Quite often in the 'roll-over' type of escape, it helps if the man on top stiffens and stays stiff. The soggy, inert holder is very often most difficult to roll off.

Escape from Tateshiho-gatame

This is an illustration of the technical escape from a hold-down. When the basic or 'Hon' version of this hold-down is applied one arm is usually left free. Whichever one it is, the escape move is simple.

Reach down with your free arm to the opponent's knee on the same side of your body and push it down. At the same time, slide your nearest leg under the opponent's leg and cross your two legs round his leg (Fig. 84). Once your two legs have joined and crossed, trapping his leg, the hold-down is technically broken and the referee will call 'Toketa!'.

However, though the hold-down is broken, the groundwork fighting does not automatically come to an end. If the person on top frees his leg, the countdown on the hold-down recommences. Once you have trapped the leg it is good contest policy to hang on to it tightly, also clasping the man on top strongly round the waist.

The trapped leg rule results from the belief that once you have trapped

Fig. 84 Escape from Tate-shiho-gatame

the leg of the man on top you will be able to roll him off. However, Toketa is called when the leg is trapped, not when he is rolled off. In training you can practise rolling the opponent off, but in contest there is the danger that the opponent may free his leg and clamp the hold-down on again.

When escaping from any hold-down you will probably have to explode in to a chain of different escape methods. For example, with Kesa-gatame, if you try to sit up, the opponent may brace one of his legs backwards, giving you a chance to trap it between your two legs. If this fails he may have momentarily relaxed his grip round your arm, giving you the opportunity to snatch it free and wriggle out of the hold-down, and so on. The opponent may, of course, be aware of all these methods and guard against them. In which case you will have no alternative but to struggle till Ippon is called. You may feel that you are in an unbreakable hold-down and want to submit after a few seconds; however, you are expected to try your utmost to break the position for the full time.

10

Common Groundwork Situations

There are a number of moves on the ground that must be learnt, which do not score but which change an inferior position into a superior one. For example, it has already been mentioned that it is bad to fight on the back with the opponent beside you and that this position can be strengthened by swinging one leg over the opponent's head and catching him between your legs. Most of the moves in this chapter are of this variety. Many of them involve the simple proposition that it is better to be leaning your weight on the opponent, than to have his on you. A basic rule of groundwork is: 'get gravity on your side'.

Getting past the legs

Often one gets trapped between the opponent's legs as he lies on his back on the ground. There is very little that can be done in this position, so instantly the choice must be made between continuing the fight on the ground or breaking it off. Breaking the fight is done by quickly standing up and lifting the opponent clear of the mat. In a contest the referee would have to call 'Matte' (break!). This is one of the rules mentioned earlier that favours the standing fighter rather than the groundwork man.

If you wish to continue on the ground, the opponent's legs must be crossed. Many inexperienced fighters try for a strangle from this position, but it is almost a complete waste of time. The rule is: 'If trapped, get past the legs'. There are several ways of doing this and one will be described.

Drive your left arm down between the opponent's encircling legs and lift him up, pushing his knees over towards his head. Next, grasp the opponent's left lapel with your right hand as high as possible and feed it into your own left hand. Keeping a strong grip with the left hand, continue bending the knees towards the head then slide your head under the opponent's right leg and move round to his right side (Fig. 85).

Fig. 85   Getting past legs

Even after you have moved round to the side, maintain the grip with your left hand, as this will prevent the opponent rolling away on to his stomach. Finally, sink your weight down on your man and go for a hold-down.

The above is an example of going under the legs, but it is also possible to go over the legs pushing one leg down and crossing over it.

Whether you go under or over the legs it is important to keep your balance. Try to keep your body upright and do not allow yourself to be toppled forward.

Turning the opponent over from between the legs

This situation is the reverse of the previous one. You have trapped the opponent between your legs, and although there are several possible arm-lock and strangle moves from this position, it is good policy to turn the opponent over on to his back, using your legs, and then go for a hold-down.

Whichever side you intend to turn the opponent over to, it is important to trap his arm on that side so that he cannot use it to brace against the turn-over. Simply catch his right sleeve with your left hand and pull it in tight to your body, or best of all encircle his upper arm with your whole arm trapping it under your arm-pit, and catch his left lapel.

Next insert your right leg between the opponent's legs and hook the instep of your right foot behind his left knee.

Drop your left leg to the mat and, using this to block his right knee, tip the opponent over sideways by lifting his left leg with your right foot and swivelling strongly to your left (Fig. 86).

Fig. 86   Turning opponent over from legs

As the opponent topples over to the side, swing into the upper position. Switch your right leg under your left, maintain your original hold and settle into a Kesa-gatame-like hold-down.

Arm-rolls

It is a common situation in groundwork for one man to be on all-fours (knees and elbows on the ground) defending against arm-locks, strangles or against being turned on to his back. With practice this can be turned into a very strong defensive position. Nevertheless a defensive position is only a defensive position and it is much better to switch to the offensive.

When you kneel on all fours on the ground the opponent may attack you from the head end, sides or rear. Whichever direction you are attacked from it is possible to catch one of the opponent's arms, roll him over and take the upper position.

One of the most common arm-rolls is done when the attacker is kneeling at your left side, resting his weight on your back. The chance for the arm-roll comes when he drops his right arm down the right side of your body. As soon as he does this, trap his arm against the side of your body with your right arm and, maintaining a very tight hold, roll over to your right (Fig. 87). Once you have rolled your man over, keep the tight hold on his arm, lean heavily against his chest and clasp his trousers on the left thigh. This will make a strong though unorthodox hold-down. If you fail with the hold-down attempt, take care to stay on top in the 'superior' position.

Fig. 87   Arm Roll

Sometimes a cagey opponent may not allow his arm to be trapped as above. Sometimes it is possible, as you crouch on all-fours, to reach under your body with your *left* hand and catch the sleeve, rolling as before.

The groundwork specialist must learn to arm-roll his opponent from whatever direction he is attacked in.

Turning an all-fours opponent over on to his back

This situation is the reverse of the previous one. Although the all-fours defensive position can be a very strong one, there are a variety of moves in the attacker's armoury. There are arm-lock and strangle possibilities and, of course, hold-downs if you can turn the man over. In general the man on top must work between all three possibilities. A useful rule is this. Go for the turn-over first (since hold-downs seem to be the most successful of groundwork moves), take it as far as you can, but watch out for arm-lock and strangle possibilities, taking them if the turn-over bogs down; if these fail, use the leverage you will have against the neck or arm (from your failed strangles, etc.) to complete the turn-over.

There is no single sure-fire technique for breaking the all-fours defensive positions, so the best advice is to make your move, whatever it is, hard and fast; it is important to act in those first few seconds that it takes the man underneath to settle into position.

One simple turn-over is as follows. Kneel at one side of the opponent and slide both arms underneath his body to catch his elbow on the far side. Having caught the elbow, pull it in sharply towards you, at the same time driving forwards with your chest into the opponent's body (Fig. 88). Roll him over on to his back and follow up with, say, Yokoshiho-gatame.

Fig. 88   Turning all-fours opponent over

Fig. 89   Straddle attack

Another good move against an opponent on all-fours is the straddle-attack. As he crouches, sit quickly on his back, wrapping both legs round his trunk. From this position you can do two things. Either iron him out flat by driving your two legs back between his so as to knock them away and flatten him, or throw yourself backwards with the man firmly held between your two legs (Fig. 89). In both cases you will need a firm grip with your hands. A good grip is to hold under both arm-pits and grasp his lapels at the front. Once you have flattened your opponent or thrown yourself backwards, there are many good chances for arm-locks and strangles and, of course, it is easier to turn him on to his back for a hold-down.

Freeing the leg

As mentioned previously, a hold-down is technically broken if the man underneath manages to catch one of the holder's legs between his. This situation often occurs in groundwork either as an escape from a hold-down or as a general defensive move. In the latter case, if the man underneath catches a leg in a general groundwork mix-up, he not only stops the possibility of being caught in a hold-down but also restricts the attacker's arm-lock and strangle moves to a considerable extent. It is necessary to know how to free the leg if caught.

Once the leg is caught the position often settles into the one shown in Fig. 90. In the illustration the man on top has started to free his leg.

The first move in the sequence is to trap the opponent's right arm. Take your right arm underneath it, then through the crook of his elbow, grasping his belt or the end of his jacket, using your left hand to feed it into your right. With this grip on the belt or jacket, clamp down tightly on the opponent's forearm. This will partially bind the opponent's arm (you are not allowed to use the belt or jacket to *completely* bind the arm) and put it out of action. This binding move is important, since the man underneath will need the use of his right arm if he is to make any sort

Fig. 90 Trapped leg

of bridging or rolling escape move. With the arm trapped you can now turn your attention to freeing the leg.

Usually your leg will be trapped above the knee and the second action you must make is to free your knee and shift the hold-down to your ankle. You do this with two simultaneous sharp actions. Push down hard against the opponent's right knee and jerk your knee free at the same time. Make these movements explosive. Once your ankle is trapped you have much more freedom to move the hips and you can do a number of follow-up moves.

First, you can bide your time, then repeat the big jerking action to free your foot. Or secondly, roll on top of the opponent and use your right foot to kick your trapped left foot free. Another method is to use the right knee to push into the top of the opponent's left thigh at the part where the thigh muscles insert into the pelvis. This can be very painful and may cause the man underneath to open his legs. Note that the rules allow this and other similar painful areas to be pushed only, not struck. These are not 'nerve' pressure points but only areas where the muscles are sensitive.

The moment that the foot is freed can be dangerous for the man on top. As the foot is released the man underneath may suddenly bridge and twist, throwing you off. However, if you keep the arm bound, as in the first move, and are careful when you release the foot, it should not be difficult to stay on top.

Once you have freed the foot, keep the opponent's arm bound, hold his left trouser leg with your left hand, and stay in position. This will constitute a hold-down.

Groundwork hints

Groundwork is largely situational with few general principles that can be applied. To be good on the ground you have to know the answer for each situation, unlike standing work where two or three throws are all you need know to fight a multitude of different opponents. However, there are some useful rules that apply in groundwork which, if grasped, may speed up the process of learning.

One of the problems of groundwork is choice. When you go into groundwork there are three possible scoring methods, and many people get into a dither, not knowing which one to go after, losing many good scoring opportunities in the process. The statistics indicate that hold-downs take eighty per cent of all groundwork scores, so in general, try for hold-downs first and take your arm-locks and strangles from that move if it fails.

This rule applies only if an arm-lock or strangle is not blatantly obvious and there for the taking. Thus when you collapse to the floor with your opponent, the first consideration if you are aiming for a hold-down, is to get your weight on him. From there you seek to tie him up in a proper hold-down, but if in the process he escapes, look for arm-lock and strangle possibilities.

Often the man who wins on the ground is the man who goes directly for a particular scoring technique. On the whole people take groundwork as it comes, going for the nearest move, so there is often a delay while they sort out in their own minds what that is. On the other hand, the man who knows in advance that he wants to make a strangle, for example, will be diving for the neck on the way to the ground. One of the reasons that the Russian Judomen scored so highly with the Juji-gatame arm-lock when they first came on the world Judo scene, is because they were single-minded about that particular move. They ignored most of the other groundwork moves.

Fighting on the ground can be divided into two:

1. fighting from underneath and
2. fighting from above

The latter is easier, since it helps to have gravity on one's side, and there is also greater freedom of movement. Fighting from above is probably the first stage in a groundwork expert's development. The next stage is to learn how to fight from underneath. The general rule here is, when underneath, curl up into a ball, keeping the arms close into the body, the knees drawn up to the stomach and the chin close to the upper chest. When defending in this position it is vital to keep in a tight ball, and not let the opponent encircle your neck with one of his arms or thread one of his arms between your arm and body. The vital rule when underneath is to keep the head and arms free. From this tight defensive position, the man underneath looks for opportunities to explode into action, either going for arm-rolls or turn-overs or arm-locks.

On the other hand, the man on top has to reverse these rules. He has got to 'iron out' the man underneath and he does this basically by spreading over the man like a blanket.

The head is often the key to prising open the opponent's position.

If his head can be moved away from the upper chest and levered right back, it becomes much more difficult for the opponent to keep his stomach muscles tightly contracted (and his legs drawn up), and often the whole position will crumble.

When fighting from the upper position it is important to maintain balance. Some people get very careless about this and lean on the opponent for support. A good groundwork man can sense this and will try to move suddenly away, causing the other man to fall, giving him an opportunity to move on top.

What often distinguishes a groundwork expert is the way he uses his whole body on the ground. Some have legs which seem to work like a second pair of arms. Quite often a strangle is done using the legs to reinforce the action of the arms. For the legs to work with the arms, it is necessary to be very supple in the lower back, hips, knees and ankles (see the section on flexibility).

Groundwork men are very tenacious fighters. They stick to their opponents like flies to fly-paper. Quite often groundwork is a war of attrition. The opponent is overwhelmed inch by inch with the attacker concentrating his force on a particular part of the opponent's body. There always comes a time in groundwork when there is a large gasp as one man gives in and lets his pent-up air out in exhaustion. The winner is often the man with the greater amount of stamina, who can keep going that tiny bit longer. For this reason it is imperative to hang on to the bitter end especially when caught in a hold-down, arm-lock or strangle. Just when you think you can resist no longer the other man collapses first.

Finally, every groundwork man must learn to cut his losses. A lot of advantage is often gained by abruptly deciding that the position is lost and switching to another. If your hold-down starts to go, do not hang on to the bitter end and perhaps get rolled over into a hold-down yourself, but suddenly switch to another move. If you find that you are prevented from rolling one way, go as far as you can, then suddenly switch the other way.

Try whatever you are doing to your maximum, then if not successful *abruptly* switch.

11

Judo Training on and off the Mat

In the Dojo

It is one thing to know and be able to demonstrate a Judo technique and quite a different matter to be able to throw a resisting opponent with it. Learning to throw resisting opponents takes some time. The main training activity of Judo is Randori, or free-fighting. Randori is a series of bouts with people of varying sizes, weights, abilities and temperaments, fought in a fairly relaxed manner with both men trying to score as often as possible with different techniques.

A Judo contest proper is decided by the first throw, submission or thirty second hold-down, and because of this sudden-death nature it is a very tense, tight fight. In Randori the tension is not there, but depending on the rivalry between the two trainees, it can get close to the real contest.

Training in a Japanese Dojo usually consists of about seventy per cent throwing Randori, twenty per cent groundwork Randori, and ten per cent warming up, suppling and strengthening exercises. The groundwork may be practised separately or as it occurs naturally from the standing work. Where space is limited it is usually done separately. A typical Japanese training session lasts about two hours and is non-stop. Rests between Randori bouts is not permitted. This sort of training is very severe and is no doubt the main reason for Japan's Judo supremacy. Since Japan has such a large Judo population, an average Dojo might contain thirty to forty Black-belts training together, and with this range of expert opposition to train against, wonderful Judo is produced. Where there is a lack of experienced opposition, the Judoka must find other methods of training.

Randori has to be guided for best results. It is useful to distinguish between club Randori and contest Randori. Club Randori should be a lighter, more relaxed form of training with the emphasis on developing technique rather than winning. Contest Randori is much tougher, tighter training and develops competitive skill. One of the shortcomings of contest Randori is that it is so tight that there is much less scope for developing technique. Since it is vital to develop a wide range of technique, club Randori should form a goodly proportion of anybody's training. Although club Randori is light and relaxed, that is not to say that it is not fast and explosive. Since winning is not the main objective, stiff defensive Judo can be dispensed with, and much more emphasis placed on attack.

Some useful rules for getting the most out of Randori are

1. practise (do Randori) with anyone, regardless of grade or size
2. make a point of practising with the person you most dislike fighting
3. practise continuously against people you are just able to throw.

Although much can be gained from practising with stronger or weaker people, you need to make your throws as often as possible to hone them to a sharp edge; people a grade or two below your own make good training partners. It is also good to train against people slightly better than yourself. To throw them you will have to 'go all out' and this training at the frontiers of your ability is what will gradually extend you.

One block to progress in your Randori, is not so much the fear of getting thrown, but of getting thrown by your equals or inferior in grade. In other words pride is a block to your training. If you are going to have a relaxed attitude to training (in order to make quicker progress) then you will have to accept the fact that you will get thrown by all and sundry. In Randori it does not matter who throws you. This is the time for experimentation when you can try all the techniques under the sun. Just bear in mind that a proper contest is the real test of your abilities.

A positive mental attitude is required when practising with people of a much higher standard or larger physique. There is a tendency to think: 'he is going to throw me anyway, so I'll let it go and not fight too hard'. The Japanese equivalent of 'Even Homer nods' is 'Even monkeys fall off trees'. This applies to expert Judoka and if you work on the expectation that somewhere along the line they will make a mistake, you will not be wrong. Everybody is throwable.

When training with people of much lower standard, they should not be thrown too hard. Apart from that, training with them presents a good opportunity to work on new techniques instead of wasting time on your main ones. Save those for the people who will stretch you.

A club session may be organised with the instructor telling you when to change to a new Randori partner, or it may be left to you to change when you want to. Sometimes the instructor may divide the class into two lines and line them up facing each other. After every five minutes the lines are reformed with one side moving up one so as to face a new partner. This way the people in the class are not given the choice of who they practise with.

Often used is pressure training, in which one man is fed a series of fresh opponents at short intervals (say about one minute) for anything up to ten minutes, but this is only for the extremely fit.

Sometimes, as part of a run-up to a major contest, a Gasshuku (pronounced Gashkoo) is held. For one or two weeks just before the event, the training is moved to a different venue, usually in the country, and training takes place, morning and afternoon and sometimes in the evening as well.

If groundwork is not practised separately, care must be taken that it is not neglected. Groundwork should occur naturally when the opportunity arises from standing work. This is the way it happens in competition. Unfortunately, groundwork opportunities are often ignored in Randori. This can become a habit. Unless you have made a really clean, powerful throw (which for competition purposes means you have won), make it a habit to follow instantly into groundwork, using the first opportunity to score. It is not necessary to spend a lot of time on the ground if you do not want to. Gain a quick submission if you can, or settle into a hold-down for about fifteen seconds, then get up. Of course, if you want to become a groundwork specialist, then spend as much time as you can on the ground.

It goes without saying that the more Randori training you do, the faster progress you will make towards your Black belt. As a rough guide, it is generally reckoned that it takes about three years, training three times a week, to reach 1st Dan. Talented people can do it in less.

Randori is the all-round Judo training par excellence. However, where it is necessary to work intensively on a particular technique, Uchi-komi, or drill training, is used. In this form of training, one technique is selected and is repeated up to one hundred times or more during some part of the session. Since being thrown a hundred times is not too comfortable for the training partner, the throw is usually performed to a stage just short of completion. However, if a crashmat or similar soft landing area is available, the throw can be completed.

At an early stage in the development of a throw, Uchi-komi may be no more than a means of remembering the technique. For example, when first shown a new technique, it is usually necessary to repeat the movement twenty or thirty times to get the feel of it. Later, when the technique becomes part of one's repertoire, it may be felt necessary to work on it to add strength, speed or accuracy. Uchi-komi is usually done on a static partner; however, once the movement can be done fast and accurately, it becomes necessary to work on the *opportunity* for the throw. If a throw is normally done against an opponent who is moving forwards, then in Uchi-komi the movement can be practised against a partner who is similarly moving forwards.

It is particularly important to pay attention to the footwork for your particular throw, that is to say not only the footwork in the throw, but the footwork leading up to the throw. Take care to practise the latter in your Uchi-komi.

Uchi-komi is unrealistic in so far as you are doing it against a co-operating partner. The final stage is to introduce resistance into your Uchi-komi. The best Judoman in the world can be stopped if the other man knows what he is doing, and it goes without saying that it is the same for Uchi-komi. What one needs here is a good partner who will give you just the right amount of resistance – starting with just a little – so as to bring the technique nearer to reality.

Maximum resistance in Uchi-komi can be gained by working against two partners. Get one to stand behind the other, clasping him around the waist, and practise your movement against the two, trying to lift or throw both bodies.

One measurable way to do this sort of skill training is to set yourself a time (say one minute), then see how many *good* repetitions of one throw you can make in that time. For the first few weeks you may only be able to fit in about thirty to forty repetitions, but with practice the number can be pushed much higher. It is essential to make sure that each move is a good one and not merely a twitch.

The crashmat (a very thick and soft falling area similar to that used by pole-vaulters) is a necessary item in every Dojo. It is extremely useful for throwing practice as mentioned previously, especially for practising those throws that nobody likes falling from, such as the big counter-throws (Ura-nage) or some of the higher throws like Kata-guruma. Making fifty throws in a row against non-resisting people is surprisingly exhausting and it indicates how strenuous Judo is. Crashmat training is a good way of building strength and stamina into one's throws.

Apart from general fighting on the ground, there are one or two special practices for groundwork. One very useful method is to practise holding and escaping. One man applies a hold-down, then gives his partner thirty seconds to escape. At the end of thirty seconds or when the hold-down is broken, the positions are reversed. Another useful practice is to build strength into 'roll-over' escapes from hold-downs. Get somebody to put a hold-down on fairly lightly, then roll them off (as in the Yokoshiho-gatame escape) fifteen times or more. As the movement gets stronger it can be practised against a tighter and tighter hold.

Groundwork moves, especially arm-locks, strangles, arm-rolls, etc., can be practised Uchi-komi style with results gained much more quickly than in standing techniques.

Groundwork training can degenerate into a slow sloth-like activity, so one useful way of speeding things up is to impose a target, a time limit and a penalty. For example, one man crouches on all fours and the other kneels close by. The man kneeling is given twenty seconds to turn the other over on to his back. If within that time he succeeds, the one underneath must do twenty-five press-ups; if he fails, *he* must do the press-ups. This is a good way to ginger up the matwork.

Whether you do standing or groundwork Uchi-komi, it is vital to make it realistic and 'alive'. Practise the movements with as near as possible the speed and accuracy you would use in Randori or contest. Otherwise you will probably be wasting your time.

In some countries where there are not sufficient numbers of people to train against in Randori, training tends to consist mostly of Uchi-komi. The sort of Judo produced tends to be strong, surprisingly strong, in the set-piece moves, but weak on the general inter-connecting moves.

Although Uchi-komi may be repetitive and boring it is probably necessary if you are contest-orientated to make it a large proportion of your training. Whereas, once, Judo training was ninety-nine per cent Randori, it is now split between, Randori, Uchi-komi and Conditioning (weight-training, etc.).

Off the mat

There are a number of reasons why it may be necessary to extend one's training outside the Dojo. The recreational Judoka who gets all he needs from a twice-weekly Randori session need look no further, but those who wish to improve their performance in order to achieve a higher grade or become a champion may well find that the local club Judo is not sufficient. The most obvious deficiency in a small club is lack of experienced opposition, and if time or distance precludes training with more and better people, other training methods have to be looked for.

There are other reasons for extending one's training outside the Dojo. Mental and physical staleness is one. It can become boring doing Judo every day of the week for years on end, and as one becomes bored the risk of injury increases.

Doing Judo alone can also make you very lop-sided. Properly done, of course, Randori is all you need, but there is always the tendency to cruise along in well-worn ruts, and an all-round balanced body and abilities are not necessarily acquired. Cruising in a rut is the greatest danger in club Judo. The body adapts to the amount of resistance it meets, and while it takes some time for the body to adapt to the strenuous demands of Judo, there comes a time when it can cope, and then it starts to cruise. From this point on, the body gets less and less from the training and this is when off-mat training becomes necessary. From the point of view of skill, the ruts, which is to say the personal techniques, are worn deeper and deeper, and it becomes more difficult to learn something new. The learner's physique often determines the techniques he uses, which results in strong points being further developed and weak points neglected. Off-mat training can broaden the range of physical qualities and hopefully the skills as well.

Whatever form of non-Judo training which is followed there are two main principles – *progressive overload* and *specificity*. Progressive overload means that whatever form of training you do, the aim must always be to do it faster, longer, more frequently or against more resistance. Although it is impossible to improve from day to day, every week or every month should see an improvement in some form or another. Records and measurements have to be kept. Do not rely on your own subjective feeling of tiredness etc. but keep a work-log of everything you do. Constantly strive to break your own records.

Specificity, and this is highly important, means training for the event, in this case Judo. It is no good training to run a four-minute mile unless you can say exactly how that ability affects your Judo. Off-mat training should always follow Judo requirements. Judo comes first, since, according to our law of specificity, you improve at Judo mainly by doing Judo. Practising another sport or form of training does not mean that you get better at Judo, unless that sport or training mirrors some aspect of Judo. Doing something with no relation to Judo may only be of value in so far as it marks a break in the training and leaves you mentally fresher afterwards.

It follows from our law of specificity that off-mat training has its limits. There comes a point of diminishing returns, when there is precious little to be gained from extra agility, endurance or strength training, and at this point increased attention must be directed to Judo techniques.

To find out what form off-mat training should take, it is necessary to look at Judo itself. In standing Judo, one holds a man at arm's length, trying to throw him, and to stop oneself being thrown. The grip is firm and the arms, shoulders and upper body move constantly against considerable resistance. There is usually constant effort to stay upright since the other man may be bending you forward from a high collar grip, and this places considerable strain on the lower back and neck. Movement around the mat is punctuated by fast bursts of activity leading to explosive throw attempts. The legs are used not only to move around the mat, but must be strong and supple enough to assume a variety of positions in throws, from supporting positions such as low squats, to actual throwing work.

The physiological requirements here are muscular endurance, muscular strength, circulo-respiratory endurance, flexibility, agility and speed.

On the ground, the activity changes slightly. Both men cling tightly to each other, movement is restricted by the proximity of the mat and is not so speedy; the neck and arms have to be strong to resist strangles and arm-locks. Flexibility is required for use of the legs. Hold-downs have to be rigidly maintained. The requirements in Ne-waza are particularly for muscular endurance, and muscular strength. Circulo-respiratory endurance and flexibility are also required.

What exactly are these qualities?

Muscular endurance means having the ability to move against moderate resistance repeated times (for example, lifting a 20 kg (45 lb) weight one hundred times). Muscular endurance in the arms and upper body is extremely important for Judo. This is sometimes known as 'local endurance'.

Muscular strength means the ability to move against strong resistance relative to yourself. Everyone has muscular strength but some have considerably less than others. An 80 kg (176 lb) weight-lifter may be able to lift 160 kg (342 lb) above his head, while an ordinary 80 kg (176 lb) man in the street may only be able to lift 40 kg or less above his head. However, muscular strength in Judo is also relative to the opponent's weight and strength. An 80 kg fighter must be able to move, with a certain amount of ease, his 80 kg (176 lb) opponent.

Circulo-respiratory endurance is the ability of the heart and lungs to service the muscles with blood to enable them to continue working at a given rate. The greater the resistance the body has to work against, the shorter time it can continue to work. Where there is no resistance other than the weight of the body and the air it moves through, activity can continue for a long time, subject to the efficiency of the heart and lungs.

Other qualities important in Judo are flexibility, agility, speed and explosion. Flexibility means being able to enjoy the *full* range of the body's movement and agility is the ability to put the body neatly and precisely where you want it.

Another quality often neglected is *relaxation*. If the body is tense it cannot move fast. It is like a car with the brakes on. The ability to loosen up when fighting, places less demand on the body and helps agility and flexibility. Hard training can raise the general level of tension in the body, so when training is over for the day it is necessary to know how to ease off. Finally, every athlete needs a good night's sleep before his next day of training.

Knowing what qualities one wants to foster, it now becomes possible to look at the various types of off-mat training and see how they can be used. It can be a big mistake to select a type of training indiscriminately without knowing in advance precisely what it is you want to train.

Weight-training is the most obvious way to build muscular strength and endurance. The resistance that the body works against can be easily calculated and increased.

Before undertaking any weight-training programme that concentrates on a particular Judo ability, it is necessary to spend some time on an all-round programme. No part of the body can be neglected since an imbalance will be created. The legs, arms, chest, stomach, upper and lower back must all be worked.

An all-round programme would be: squats for the legs, bench-press and bent-over rowing for the arms, upper back and chest, sit-ups for the stomach and dead lift for the lower back.

In squats, the Judoka squats up and down with a weight on the shoulders. In the bench-press, the person lies on a bench and lowers a weight to his chest and pushes it away again. In bent-over rowing the person stands bent over from the waist, and pulls a weight to his chest and down again. In sit-ups the person lies on his back with his feet secured and sits up, and in dead lift the weight is lifted from the floor using only the back, with straight legs and straight hanging arms.

Weight-training is usually done according to a formula:

$$\text{number of Sets} \times \text{number of Repetitions} \times \text{Poundage.}$$

If muscular strength is the aim, the poundage should be high and the sets and repetitions low. For example, if the aim is to build very strong legs, repetitions are low, one to three, repeated three times using the maximum poundage that the legs can take for that performance. Often a pyramid system is used, that is progressively loading the bar as the sets increase. Thus the trainee, knowing that his maximum weight for one squat is 91 kg (200 lb), would load the bar at 86 kg (190 lb), put it across his shoulders and squat three times. For the next set, he would load the bar to 88 kg (195 lb) and try to squat three times (he might only do two) and for the third set he would load 91 kg (200 lb) and try three squats, possibly only doing it once. The training continues over the weeks until he can do each set with three repetitions, and then he changes the loading on the bar, starting at around 88 kg (195 lb) and finishing at 93–95 kg (205–210 lb). In this way the poundage is gradually pushed higher.

When muscular endurance is the aim, the repetitions and sets should be high and the poundage correspondingly low. Since a muscular endurance is highly important in Judo, four sets of fifteen to twenty repetitions is recommended.

Thus our hypothetical trainee who can lift a maximum of 91 kg (200 lb) in the squat, might find he can only lift about 54 kg (120 lb) fifteen times repeated in four sets. Once he finds what he can do at that number of repetitions and sets, he trains until he can do the full number of repetitions per set and then he increases the poundage. This number of sets and repetitions is very demanding, but so is Judo itself, especially contest Judo.

Training for speed and explosion can also be worked into the weight-training. When you are training for muscular strength, and it is all you can do to move the weight at all, you will not be able to move the weight faster, but as the weight gets lighter (when training for muscular endurance) the choice is whether to do the repetitions fast or slowly and here the choice should be fast. This, of course, places more demands on the body and will affect the Sets by Repetitions by Poundage formula.

The faster the weights are moved, the more explosive becomes the action; however, a more total explosion can be worked at in weight-training by doing such exercises as the snatch (taking the weight above one's head in a single movement from the ground), using either a bar or dumbell. Dumbell work is especially advised for Judo since one arm has often to work alone or do more work than the other.

Training for recovery is highly important in Judo, and this can be done in weight-training. Between sets there is a rest, and also between the different exercises. It is important not to rest too long. Fix a time between the bursts of work and stick to it. If possible, shorten the gap until the work becomes virtually continuous. Done this way it will be extremely tiring, but eventually the body will learn to cope and the toughest Judo will become easier.

For Judomen new to weight-training, it is important to remember the principle of specificity. Judo comes first and a measure of skill (up to about 1st Dan) should be acquired first before embarking on extra training. Then the first two months should be spent on an all-round weight-training programme which works all parts of the body, using moderate sets and repetitions (three sets of eight to ten repetitions) done at medium speed and with sufficient rest in between. This will accustom the body to the new form of training and prepare it for the harder work ahead.

Next, training for muscular strength and muscular endurance can be combined or done separately, alternating between them from one training session to the next, or spending a few weeks on one then a few weeks on the other.

Remember to combine speed and recovery work in your training as you get stronger. Finally, specific exercises for Judo skills can be worked on. These depend on what techniques you use on the mat. Weight trainers often tend to avoid the exercise they hate doing the most. This may indicate a weak spot in their physiques. Make sure that your overall training programme includes work on all parts of the body especially the legs.

Always bear in mind what you are training for. The time may come when your strength and endurance are sufficient and then you will go on a *maintenance* programme, which would mean doing the same thing but much less frequently. From this point on, more attention should be paid to developing Judo skills. Do not get side-tracked into body-building or weight-training routines. Your aim is not to have an impressive physique or lift record poundages above your head.

Running is the next most obvious form of training, used by most athletes to supplement their sport. Here the aim is to work on stamina or circulo-respiratory endurance. Whatever movement the body makes, the heart and lungs have to service the muscles for that movement with oxygenated blood. The greater the resistance, the faster the movement, and the more frequently it is made, the greater the demand placed on the heart and lungs. Thus the heart will increase its work rate as the body moves from walking to running, to sprinting. The faster the speed and the greater the resistance, the shorter the time the heart and body muscles can continue. The muscles contain a store of energy which they can use up before extra demands are placed on the lungs and heart. Thus a sprinter covers one hundred metres on one breath, but after that the muscles cry out for newly oxygenated blood and the breathing grows more and more violent.

A Judo match consists of up to ten minutes non-stop leg work, with arms moving against constant heavy resistance, punctuated by violent bursts of throwing activity. Japanese scientists who have pulse-rated Judo say that the average pulse rate for Randori is about 180 beats per minute and of course a Judo *contest* is even more strenuous. Judo is an extremely arduous activity.

All forms of continuous activity, such as running, swimming and cycling, specifically work the heart and lungs because they are continuous. Weight-training may be very hard work for the heart but in between sets the pulse rate falls so that the average pulse rate for the whole training session may be quite low. This applies to all stop-start activities such as tennis, football and squash. To gain circulo-respiratory endurance it is necessary to do something which raises the heart rate and keeps it there for a certain time, and this is where such activities as running and swimming are invaluable.

Before running indiscriminately, Judo requirements must be looked at. What, for example, is the value of running 10 km (six miles)? It might take thirty to forty minutes to run this distance with a pulse rate of about 160 per minute. If the extra fitness is for competition, then one might require the heart and lungs to stand up to ten minutes' activity with a pulse rate of 180 per minute. Thus, while it might be pleasant to run every day for twenty to thirty minutes, gaining the advantages of fresh air and sunshine, it would probably be better to train at running for ten minute periods as fast as possible, trying to push the heart rate higher. The ten minutes could be spent running at a fast even pace, or spent alternating sprinting and jogging. When sprinting is incorporated into the running, the extra elements of speed and explosion are also worked on.

The type of interval training practised by the British Judo team before the Munich Olympics, when it took three medals, consisted of sets of sprints, carrying weights in each hand, over an eight to ten minute period. This training strengthened their hearts much more than Judo could, and contributed towards their extreme fitness and success.

Finally, if one is training for a big championship, championship conditions could be simulated! The contestants fight a match every hour for maybe eight hours, so muscular endurance or circulo-respiratory endurance training could be done for ten minutes every hour during the day. Training carried to these lengths would probably be only for the potential Olympic athlete.

Judo throws such as Uchi-mata and Seoinage require considerable *flexibility*, as does groundwork. There is a tendency to regard stiffness in the joints and tight muscles as some sort of inherited disability. This is not so, and anybody can loosen up to a considerable degree. Some parts of the body take much longer than others to loosen, but with patience full range of movement can be brought back to all joints and the muscles servicing them can be stretched.

The common and mistaken way of loosening up is to do a few 'jerks', such as touching the toes, as part of a warm-up routine. Unfortunately, jerking the muscles produces a protective shortening reaction.

The way to loosen up is to stretch slowly as far as it is possible to go comfortably, hold the position, breathing normally for up to thirty seconds, then, still as relaxed as possible, move a little further and hold for another thirty seconds. This can be done twice more (three sets in all) and repeated patiently over three to twelve months. Gradually the joints and muscles will loosen up and more and more stretch will be gained. Patience and relaxation is the keynote.

Areas that tend to stiffen in Judo are the lower back, hips and shoulders. The lower back especially needs to be kept loose.

Useful exercises for Judo are the front bend, back bend and sideways twist. For the front bend, sit on the floor with legs together, stretched out in front. Lean forwards, grasp the ankles, and using the above method, eventually try to rest the chest along the thighs, keeping the legs straight, the backs of the knees touching the floor. At first it may not be possible even to touch the toes, but gradually you will get there. Remember the chest is laid along the thighs, *not* the head dipped to the knees. A similar exercise can be done with the legs spread wide apart. These forward bends will really stretch the lower back.

For the back bend, lie face down on the floor, legs together and straight with the palms of the hands on the floor under each shoulder. Then, breathing out, straighten the arms, lifting the upper body away from the ground but keeping the hips on it. Straighten the arms as far as possible and *do not hunch the shoulders*. Finally, lift the head up and look at the ceiling. This will produce an excellent stretch in the lower back, an area which takes a lot of strain in Judo, and which can suffer a certain amount of misalignment and damage. Remember to keep the hips on the floor and stretch the toes backwards.

For the sideways twist, sit on the floor as for the forward bend. Lift the right knee up, and, twisting round to the left, place the left hand on the floor behind you as far round as you can. Next, lift the right elbow up and placing it against the inside of the right knee, use it as base to push off to get more twist round to the left. Use both arms to maintain maximum twist. Repeat the other way. The sideways twist is very useful for relieving lower back ache.

A final exercise for the shoulders and rib-cage, which tend to stiffen from all the hard work the upper body does in Judo, is to take the Judo belt, and hold about a three foot length of it out in front of the body, stretched tight between the two hands. Then, keeping the belt taut, lift it up and over the head to touch behind your back, keeping the arms straight during the whole movement. This exercise is easily done with a wide grip, but the aim is to get the hands gradually closer and closer together. A good test of shoulder flexibility is to be able to clasp the hands together, behind the back between the shoulder-blades.

A few minutes spent stretching the body before and after every training session is highly recommended. Hatha Yoga is a very good form of stretching exercise for Judo.

In modern contest Judo *agility* is extremely important. Many Judo throws are complex movements requiring great co-ordination. In addition, many Judo men are able to escape from being thrown by twisting or somersaulting in the air in mid-throw. As some people have a tendency to freeze when upside down in the air, it can be of great advantage to learn some basic gymnastic and trampoline moves.

Expert tuition in these activities should be sought in the gymnasium, but as a rough guide the aspiring champion should be able to do cart-wheel, forward head spring and hand spring, front somersault and back somersault and back hand spring. All these moves can be done on the trampoline, adding twisting movements, which are especially useful for Judo.

Relaxation, like flexibility, tends to be a neglected area of training. A tense body reacts slowly and consumes energy. A more or less permanent tension may result from hard training, especially from competition, with the psychological problems of winning and losing. Like stiffness, tension is not something you have to live with. There are methods of losing it, though patience is required.

There are a number of methods, ranging from simple relaxation exercises to meditation to bio-feedback machines. It must be remembered, however, that relaxation is an ability acquired like flexibility or agility. It takes time to acquire but is very worthwhile.

A simple relaxation exercise is to set aside a regular period between training sessions. Find a soft, warm surface to lie on, take your shoes off, loosen any tight clothes, and lie down. Exclude harsh light from your eyes, get warm, then try to consciously let everything go. Start with the feet and relax each part of the body systematically up to the crown of the head. First become aware of each part of the body and then let it relax. Another helpful tip is to rest the hands on the stomach and just be aware of them rising and falling with the breathing. Think of something pleasant though not exciting and practise regularly for ten minutes at a time. Gradually you can learn the ability to let go and relax easily and quickly at will.

If meditating, sit with the legs crossed or in the Japanese kneeling style. You may also use a chair. Keep the back straight and chin pulled in slightly. Do not try to *do* anything. Listen to the rise and fall of the breathing, be aware of the stomach moving in time with it. Alternatively, let the thoughts rise and fall, avoiding complicated chains of thought. Just let each individual thought grow and die. Another method is to intone to yourself a sound such as Om (it rhymes with 'home') and let the whole of it fill your body – become the sound itself. In meditation you will relax because that is part of the process, but more important you will get an understanding of why you became tense in the first place and when this is realised a much deeper fundamental relaxation can be attained.

Some scientific studies have shown that the meditative state is more relaxed than deep sleep and more refreshing. With practice, facility can be gained.

A more recent development on this front is the bio-feedback machine which registers tension electronically and gives you a method of reducing it, using the machine itself.

Remember the general principles of off-mat training:

1. Progressive overload. Do it faster, longer, more frequently and against more resistance. Keep records.
2. Specificity. Train specifically for Judo. Always ask yourself how your training relates to Judo itself.
3. Make the distinction between muscular strength, muscular endurance and circulo-respiratory endurance, and train accordingly.
4. Do not ignore flexibility, agility and relaxation – these will help to expand your technical range.
5. Always try to incorporate the factors of speed, explosion and recovery in your training.

A well trained Judoka is not a shuffling Frankenstein powerhouse but a fast, agile, supple, explosive, strong and durable athlete.

12

Contest Judo

Contest Judo should be a feature of any Judoka's career. It is traditionally regarded both as the means for testing one's ability and as an important learning situation. In addition it is usually the path to a higher coloured belt. Grades in Judo are mainly awarded for ability rather than knowledge and this ability is tested in contest. And, of course, there are now many people who only do Judo to become champions.

Contest Judo is different from Randori Judo. First, it is fought for only one winning point, which makes it much tighter and tenser than club Judo, and secondly, it is fought under certain limitations such as rules and weight categories.

Like any other form of activity, one becomes good at contest Judo by doing it. So the first recommendation with contest Judo is to go in for every contest that is available. This is the only way to get the feel of the big event, the nerves and the different settings. Never miss a contest, however unimportant.

Like any other sport it is essential to know the rules before you compete. A contest lost through ignorance of the rules is sheer carelessness. If necessary, become a referee, or attend the courses on the rules that are run for referees. That way you will learn what they are looking for.

Always accept a referee's decision. It is a fact of Judo (and probably all sports) that there are bad referees and bad decisions. Bear in mind that bad decisions work both ways. One can give you the gold medal as well as take it away. Accept the decision, but bear in mind the coach's golden words to his protegé who claimed he was robbed, 'you should'a buried him'. There is no argument if the opponent submits from an arm-lock or strangle, and none if you flatten him with a one hundred per cent throw.

Everyone is nervous before a contest. To a nervous newcomer to contest Judo this might not be very obvious, especially when he looks at the apparently calm, big names around him. Beneath their calm exterior there is a real turmoil going on. In fact, it is probably safe to say that without pre-contest nerves a good performance is impossible. How you feel before a contest is no indication of how you will do in it. One famous American runner was sick every time before he broke the world record.

There are a number of ways to approach contest Judo. In Boxing, it is said that there is the fighter and the boxer, and similarly in Judo, there is the technician and the mauler. These two stylistic approaches to Judo are very obvious in contest. On the one hand, there is the rough, strong, aggressive mauler and on the other, there is the fast, accurate, supple technician. For best contest results, it is necessary to be able to switch between these styles. Sometimes the best way to fight a mauler is as a technician, and sometimes it is possible to out-maul the mauler. When training, alternate between going for the swift, clean, deadly, accurate score and the 'grab-anything-that-moves, knock 'em-down-anyhow' style. Experience will show how many people cannot cope with one style or the other and this will then prove very useful in contest.

An alternative style to practise in training is the 'lurker'. The rules on passivity work against this style but scope for it does exist. Briefly, it means being able to switch from the forward aggressive style to a lurking counter-throw or counter-attack style. You can either wait or invite a chance for a straight counter-throw, or fire off your own attack the moment the other man starts to attack. The efficacy of changing style was ably demonstrated in the Munich Olympics. One fighter 'powered' his way through to the final of his weight class. On the way he beat a Russian, but because of the Repechage system had to fight him again in the final. In the final he continued his strong aggressive style, but the Russian switched and became a lurker. The switch paid off, with the Russian making a strong counter-throw to win the gold medal.

It is vital to be able to change your style of fighting.

Another general rule for contest is to have an answer for everything.

Never merely defend, but always try to do something, no matter how desperate. For example, there is a strong contest grip with which the attacker controls the opponent's head by holding strongly at the back of his collar, bending and pinning him down. The stock reaction to this is for the controlled man to pull away from the grip as far as he can, or break it. This, of course, is what the attacker wants and expects and then he uses this reaction. Instead of pulling away from this sort of control, work within it by trying to pick the opponent up with a waist grip or grab his legs. However novel a situation you find yourself in, do something. Never just stand and wait to see what will happen.

One absolutely important rule is to avoid the 'stalemate'. The usual pattern of a contest is a brief flurry of grip fighting, then a quick settling down into a strong mutual grip. Once settled into this stalemate, it becomes ten times more difficult to score. A lot of scoring is done when one man manages to free his upper body, even for just a split second, from his opponent's restricting grip, and throw in an attack. It is not necessary to avoid the stalemate grip all the time, but at frequent intervals an 'eruption' must take place and the whole of the opponent's grip must be shattered. He will quickly get it back again, so an attack must be part of the eruption. Alternatively, breaks will naturally occur during a contest, for example when both fighters go out of the contest area and the referee calls them back to the middle to resume the fight. The resumption of a grip is a prime opportunity for scoring and should be used.

General advice for a contest is to make the first attack, and put the attacks together in twos. Psychological domination of the opponent is all part of the game, and though there may be no technical advantage in making the first attack, it helps to gain the upper hand psychologically. 'Freezing' is another contest problem. Launching the first attack helps to get you 'unfrozen' earlier, and making the attacks in pairs helps overcome the tendency to make single, cramped attacks from a frozen defensive position.

One way to upset the opponent is to break the rhythm of his attacks. Many people have to wind themselves up for an attack, and if just before the attack you throw in a fairly light ankle-sweep, for example, they often have to start all over again. Attacks often come at regular intervals, and some opponents can be controlled in this way for quite some time.

It helps to spot the rhythm of an opponent's attacks by watching him in operation against somebody else. People tend to have a set pattern of attacks, or idiosyncratic moves which give an indication of what is coming next, and these can be spotted in advance. Of course, knowing these facts is never the same as feeling (and surviving) them in contest, but every little bit helps.

For your own confidence, try to go into every contest knowing that you have trained twice as hard as everybody else, which of course means that you *must* train twice as hard as everybody else. Also have faith in the belief that nobody is impregnable. The toughest, most brilliant Judomen can and do go down to the silliest, most unexpected moves. If you sincerely believe this, you will throw them. Never think of defeat, only of victory.

If a contest is coming up at short notice, it is said that rapid progress in contest ability can be made by working on counter-throws and groundwork.

When you go in for a contest you must be technically well equipped. Your first weapon should be one big super-throw of which you are confident, of which the opposition is frightened, and with which you know you can score Ippon. Winning by scores of less than 10 points is the hard way to do it. It goes without saying that to win ten contests in the first minute with Ippon is better than to win ten contests fought for five minutes with a Koka (3-points), especially when the eleventh contest is the final of a big championship.

Do not be content to have a big throw that scores only miserable three or five point scores. Work on your major technique, use video tape to see yourself in action as often as you can, get advice on your throw, read about it, live it and sleep it, and develop something that will flatten everybody.

To complement your big throw, a throw in the opposite direction is very useful. Next, if you can, learn a third throw to one of the sides, possibly a left-handed one (if you are a right-hander). Ideally you should be able to throw your opponent in any direction, but of course it takes a long time to acquire a large repertoire of throws.

On the ground, go for a hold-down in the first instance unless a perfect chance for a strangle or arm-lock offers itself, and then take your arm-locks or strangles from your attempts to hold.

Some contests are much too important to experiment in, but use the minor ones as an opportunity to try out some of your ideas. Keeping a contest record is also very useful. Over a period the record will show what your Ippon rate is, and what techniques you are not scoring with.

Self-deception is a danger to be constantly watched against. Some people are convinced they are champions but somehow manage to avoid confronting the fact that they never win the gold medal. Excuses abound (bad referees, injuries etc.) but never the golds.

A Judo contest demands absolute concentration for the full length of the contest, and this is extremely difficult, especially when the going gets rough. When the contest is very evenly matched, fight for every last advantage and to the bitter end. Train to win with an Ippon in the first minute, but be prepared to have to win with a Koka (3-points) in the last two seconds. Against 'sticky' opposition, that is very strong, difficult-to-throw, awkward men, be prepared to win by being the superior attacker (where there is no score the one who has attacked most wins). This means non-stop attacking and being superfit.

It is essential not to be too predictable in contest. For example, a throw can be responded to in several ways; you can block, avoid or counter it. Whatever you do, do not make the same response, vary them. Similarly try to develop a few tricks. A trick is something that will only work once on the same man. It should be anything unusual which, given sufficient surprise, might work. Examples of tricks are leg grabs, standing strangles and arm-locks, take-downs, in fact anything outside the run of the mill throws.

Try to make your actual main-throw attacks unpredictable. Adopt a neutral stance and grip – one that shows nothing of your intentions – and try to make your throws appear from nowhere. This means paying attention to any small giveaway preparatory moves or twitches and eliminating them.

Do not enter a contest as an over-trained drudge. If rest and relaxation are built into your training programme you should be able to turn up on the day, bright-eyed, full of bounce and expectation and raring to go. This sort of spirit can rip apart a superior man who has trained himself into the ground. The fact that a contest is decided by an Ippon there and then means that the inspired, bolt from the blue can topple anybody. Compete with the expectation that this could be your gold medal day but be prepared to come back ten times more if it is not. The luck of the draw, injuries, and the constant turn-over of the top men have a lot to say in who gets the gold. The best man is not always the winner but if you compete long enough, the breaks go your way.

Injuries are the bane of every contest Judoman. More often than not the injuries may not be very serious in themselves but just enough to make training unpleasant. Swollen fingers and bruised toes or feet come in this category. If you stop training till they disappear you may rarely step on the mat. To a certain extent they have to be endured if you are aiming for the heights. Of course, expert medical care must be sought for all these injuries. Look for a good sports medicine department of a hospital because it is quite likely that the best advice you will get from your own doctor is to give up Judo. Osteopaths are often very knowledgeable about joint injuries and are worth a visit.

Knees cause special training problems. A wrenched knee may require several weeks' rest before it feels better again. What often happens is that the knee is given about three weeks' rest, is wrenched again within minutes of stepping back on the mat and the injury is made much worse, requiring a much longer period of rest or an operation.

Surgical treatment of knees is getting more and more sophisticated but it can be avoided if the newly injured knee is given sufficient rest and then properly strengthened before training recommences.

Lower backs can be injured from incorrectly applied throws. Apart from stiffness in the area the injury may not be that apparent but may lead to worse troubles later on. Expert medical care is required for this but the problem can be avoided by regular suppling exercises for that part of the body.

Cauliflower ears come in the same category as finger and toe injuries. The best way to get rid of a cauliflower ear is to have it drained by a doctor, then rest from Judo till the ear is back to normal. If you recommence Judo before it is, the slightest tap on the ear will cause it to balloon up again. There are some appliances that may be worn to protect the tender ear but they are mostly cumbersome and not very effective. The aspiring Judoka may well have to put up with a hardened cauliflower ear.

Attitudes to being strangled unconscious vary. The Japanese largely disregard them and continue training shortly after they regain consciousness. Medical research is required here. Probably the best course is to take a rest until you feel *completely* recovered; then carry on.

If you get thrown very hard and your head hits the mat, there is always the likelihood of concussion. If you feel at all unwell after a very heavy throw, take a rest or leave the session. In cases of heavy concussion you may not be in a position to take action yourself and it is up to the instructor to look after you.

Joint dislocations are easily treated, requiring suitable manipulation by the doctor or osteopath and a period of rest afterwards.

There is an ancient art allied with most of the martial arts, called Katsu, which includes revival techniques and bone setting. A real Katsu expert is very useful to have in a Dojo but very much to be avoided is the have-a-go amateur (which includes Japanese high-graded Judoka) who rush to help after an injury. If in doubt go to properly qualified medical people.

Finally, for those more traditionally minded, I include two ancient Samurai formulae. The three main causes of defeat are said to be Futanren, Mikuzure and Kiki-oji. Futanren is simply 'insufficient training'. Mikuzure means 'to see and crumble' and means being mentally defeated by the appearance of an opponent, such as his size or manner. Kiki-oji means to 'hear and tremble' and means to be defeated by an opponent's reputation. After any contest it is useful to reflect on which of these categories one's defeat is attributable to.

The formula for victory in battle is: Ichi-gan, Ni-soku, San-tan, Shi-riki. This means, 'first – eyes, second – legs, third – courage, fourth – strength'. 'Eyes' means having all the qualities of the eyes such as awareness, concentration, care and 'legs' means having strong and durable legs or perhaps what we would call stamina. Paraphrased, the formula might read, 'be careful, have lots of stamina, fight like a tiger, and be as strong as a bull'.

13

Kata

When Jigoro Kano first founded his school of Judo, training proceeded on two main fronts, namely the physical and the intellectual. The intellectual training consisted of Kogi (lectures) and Mondo (question and answer sessions). Kano gave frequent lectures about all aspects of Judo, and was always ready to answer questions and test his students' knowledge by asking the odd penetrating question.

The physical training was of two sorts and equal stress was placed on both. Daily training consisted of Randori (free-fighting) and Kata (pre-arranged movement sequences).

A few years after the inception of the Kodokan, such was the inflow of students that it became difficult to concentrate on both Kata and Randori and Randori gained greater prominence. It was always Kano's intention, however, that Kata should be given great stress, and during the Kodokan's first thirty years or so he devised many Kata, of which seven are still part of the system of Judo. It is perhaps safe to say that no self-respecting Judo Black belt can call himself an expert until he has mastered all seven Kata.

The Kata are the 'memory-banks' of Judo. They were devised so as to give the trainee the widest possible training in the techniques and principles of Judo which would not necessarily be understood or practised in Randori alone.

It is impossible to illustrate the Kata in one short chapter since they contain 129 techniques in all, but a brief description of each will be given and an account of their underlying principles and aims.

Nage no Kata   (the Kata of throws)

This is one of the two Randori Kata, the other one being the Katame no Kata. The techniques used in these two Kata are all allowed in free-fighting, with the exception of one leg-lock at the end of the Katame no Kata.

The Nage no Kata consists of fifteen throws, divided into five groups of three. Each group illustrates three throws of a particular type. The groups are, in order:

1. arm-throws (te-waza)
2. hip-throws (koshi-waza)
3. leg-throws (ashi-waza)
4. front-sacrifice throws (ma-sutemi-waza)
5. side-sacrifice throws (yoko-sutemi-waza).

Each throw is done to the right and the left and in a strict pre-arranged sequence of movements.

One of the obvious advantages of training with this Kata is that the practitioner learns to do a wide variety of throws to the right and left, whereas if he were left to his own devices in free-fighting he might only learn two or three techniques on one side. The point of this Kata is not that fifteen techniques are practised willy-nilly but that the throws are set in highly significant grip and movement situations. This Kata is a core of essential Randori information.

Katame no Kata   (the Kata of groundwork)

This Kata consists of three groups of five techniques. The first group consists of Hold-downs, the second Strangles and the third of Joint-locks. Apart from the last technique which is a knee-lock, these techniques are all commonly found in groundwork free-fighting.

Kime no Kata   (the Kata of decisive techniques)

It is in this and some of the other non-Randori Kata that the Atemi, or striking techniques of Judo are to be found. Jigoro Kano had always included kicking and punching in Judo, but had found that they were difficult to do in free-fighting, especially when combined with throws and groundwork. He experimented with Atemi in an attempt to devise a free-fighting method, but never came up with anything satisfactory. Probably it will always prove difficult to mix striking and grappling (catching hold) techniques, since it tends to turn into a messy free-for-all. Nevertheless, the Judo instructor is not precluded from trying to devise a method of training along these lines for his students.

The Kime no Kata is a mix of all the different types of Judo techniques and is divided into two parts, the first done kneeling Japanese style, and the second done standing up. The first part consists of eight techniques and is a series of defences against various attacks, including two with a knife. In most of them, the defender finally defeats his attacker with an Atemi strike to a vital spot.

The second part consists of twelve techniques, many of them similar to those in the first part, but done standing up. In addition to the combination of striking, strangling and joint-locking techniques, the final two defences are against an attacker with a Japanese sword.

From a Western point of view the kneeling techniques of the first part are of limited use, though they might be relevant for people sitting in chairs. Though the techniques are limited in number, they are meant to be representative, covering most of the defence situations. In later years the Kodokan, perhaps recognising the need to up-date this Kata, brought out a Kata-like series of self-defence moves, which it called Goshinjitsu.

When practised, this Kata must be done realistically. The attacker must really attack and not just go through the motions. Like all the other Kata, it is meant to be practised countless times so that the attacker and the defender harmonise in synchronised, flowing and realistic movement.

Ju no Kata   (the Kata of non-resistance)

This Kata was devised for a number of reasons. Kano saw that Judo, as practised on a soft mat with special clothes had limitations, so he put together a Kata that could be practised without special clothes or on a special surface.

Furthermore, from the physical training point of view he saw that Randori especially, when practised vigorously, tended to shorten the muscles and produce unbalanced physiques. So in this Kata he included a number of movements that would stretch and relax the muscles. He also indicated that the movements should be done in a relaxed, soft, slow manner, and this also gave scope for the weaker and older members of the Kodokan to practise their Judo. Not only did he regard it as useful for these people, but he saw it as a good way to channel the unco-ordinated and violent movements of the rougher and higher spirited element.

The movements are not just a series of calisthenics, but are all basic Judo moves, illustrating the principles of attack and defence.

The Kata consists of three sets of five movements and is a series of Judo pushing, pulling, bending, stretching, turning and twisting actions. None of the throwing movements is completed.

Koshiki no Kata   (the old-style Kata)

This is a Kata from the Kito style of Ju-jitsu of which Kano was a master. It was devised as a Kata for what was known as 'Yoroi-kumiuchi', or 'armoured grappling'. When the ancient Samurai fought on the battle-field, they wore armour which, though light by European standards, was still heavy and cumbersome. Kicking and punching was ruled out because of the armour, so a series of technically limited throwing techniques was devised for the hand to hand combat. This was called Yoroi-kumiuchi. The movements are performed slowly in imitation of armoured movements, and the whole Kata is simple and of narrow technical content.

Apart from the techniques which illustrate the throwing principles of Judo, the Kata was used as a vehicle for training Hontai. This is a state of mind that was highly valued in the Kito Ju-jitsu school. It means having an immovable mental centre, no matter what is happening around one. This is said to be the basis of true victory. Thus while the Kata is done, the practitioners must be fully aware of what is happening mentally.

The Kata is done in two parts, Omote and Ura (front and rear) and the mental attitude to each is different.

In the Omote part of fourteen techniques, the practitioner must forget about the opponent, and about winning or losing. He must con-centrate on himself, keeping his mind still and peaceful. In addition, he must be aware of the rise and fall of his attention with each tech-nique, being aware of the breaks in the movements.

In the second part, the action must flow like water in a flood, with no breaks between the individual techniques. The seven techniques should be fast, strong and continuous and the mind must flow with them.

Itsutsu no Kata (the Kata of five movements)

The movements in this Kata are expressions of Judo movements likened to the movements of water.

The first is likened to flowing water, which, though by nature very soft, can in the end disintegrate the largest rock. Thus, in Judo, no matter how strong an opponent is, one's force rationally used in incessant attacks can overcome him.

The second movement is likened to an angry wave, symbolising the intensity and violence of a preliminary attack. If one confronts a mighty attack from a much larger opponent one will get knocked down, in much the same way as an enormous wave will sweep aside anything in its path. But if one turns aside from the direct violence, not only can one escape defeat, but that force can be turned back against itself and defeated.

The fourth movement is likened to the suction of a large wave which has just crashed on the beach and is rolling back. If, when the opponent is about to attack, one concentrates one's maximum power in a single unfaltering attack, the opponent's solid defence can be smashed and he can be overwhelmed.

The fifth movement is likened to a giant wave which is about to wash over one. In the same way that one can avoid the force of a wave by diving under it, so one can defeat a vast opposing and unavoidable force by diving right in and under it at the very last moment, staking all on the action.

This Kata is said to be one of the most difficult to perform, largely because of its symbolic nature.

Seiryoku-Zenyo Kokumin Tai-iku no Kata (the Kata of the people's physical education in the principle of best use of mind and body)

This Kata has two functions. The first, as its name suggests, is as a series of calisthenics to be done before Randori. The other is to make the Judoka practise Atemi, which he would not otherwise do much of in Randori.

Kano says in his only book on Judo (*Judo Kyohon*), 'it is a principle of physical education to prepare for harsh exercise by doing gentle exercise and to do balanced exercises before possible one-sided exercise'.

He then went on to recommend this balanced form of warming up exercise to be done before Randori. However, he was keen that the Judoka who mostly practised Randori should not forget Atemi, so he made these exercises in Atemi form.

This Kata is very much like a Karate Kata, and is evidence of the fact that Kano included striking techniques in his Judo.

The Kata is in two parts. The first part is done solo and the second with a partner. The first part consists of a sequence of twenty-eight moves. Twenty-three of them are striking techniques with the hand, and five are kicks. The second part, consisting of ten techniques, is a series of parries and counter punches to various attacks and grips. Although this is an official Kata, it is very rarely done, which probably reflects the difficulty the Kodokan had in meshing striking and grappling techniques.

It is important to make all the movements in the various Kata meaningful and alive. They must be practised time and time again with full concentration. Not only must the practitioner be fully aware of his own movements but he must be aware of those of his partner too. When a Kata is done properly it is as if an invisible thread joins the two men and is never allowed to slacken.

14

Self-Defence

One of the three traditional objectives of Judo is Shobu. The Japanese dictionary defines this as 'victory and defeat'. Kano explained this as 'techniques that allow one to physically control, and not be controlled by, others'. Control he defined as 'having the ability to kill, maim or restrain another.' This point has been made because, in recent years, some have claimed that Judo has nothing to do with self-defence, being just a sport. Judo is simply what you make it.

The *complete* system of Judo is very useful for self-defence. On the one hand there are the Kata that instruct and train the practitioner in a wide variety of throws, joint-locks, kicks and punches in different situations, and foster the appropriate mental attitude. And on the other hand there is the Randori training method that adds the cement to the bricks.

The free-fighting builds strength, stamina, courage, ability to endure pain, plus the skill to throw at will, and to crack on arm-locks and strangles. The free-fighting also gives those elusive qualities of intuition, experience, self-confidence and the ability to act quickly. Any self-defence system that does not have a free-fighting training method is incomplete and artificial.

However, probably most people who do Judo only practise free-fighting, and this by no means makes them good at self-defence. The Randori must be modified very slightly to make it useful in this respect.

First, you must constantly be aware of the other person. Always keep your opponent within your field of vision, and never turn your back on him. The next important thing to remember is that in self-defence-orientated Randori, the fight starts at finger-tip touching distance. Many Judoka are used to free-fighting only after the grips have been taken on each other's jackets. If they did this in self-defence it would make them vulnerable to punches and kicks. In good contest Judo, the fight starts when the two contestants can touch each other, at finger-tip touching distance, and this is the way it should be played in Randori, especially if self-defence training is in mind. Once the grip has been snatched from this distance, it should become habit to throw in a quick attack. The meandering, casual attacking style of some Judoka is no good for self-defence. Attacks must be sudden and sharp with lots of grip-breaking.

Having got his grip in this situation, the Judoka has an enormous advantage. Not only can he do his Judo but he can control the other man by the simple expedient of keeping him off balance. A man off-balance is unable to punch or kick.

The Judo itself must be done slightly differently. A technique that relies on a special jacket grip, for example, might not be much good in the streets on a thinly-clad assailant. It is good training to practise Judo occasionally without jackets. If you can throw a man who is not wearing a jacket you should be able to throw him in the street.

It is also necessary to focus your techniques. That is to say, you must be capable of intensifying your throw so as to be able to put your man down for the count if necessary. Throws that roll the opponent to the floor are no good. Beware of using Sacrifice throws (Sutemi-waza) since it is a general rule of self-defence to stay on your feet. Arm-locks need to be cracked on if they are to be effective, since, if you do not put the arm out of action, the attacker can carry on attacking.

Of course, intensified throws, arm-locks and strangles carried to their limits, are not for club Randori but only for situations in which you are *forced* to defend yourself.

In addition to the above combat-style of Randori, you must also practise many times the non-Randori Kata, especially the Kime no Kata, Koshiki no Kata, Ju no Kata and the Seiryoku–Zenyo Kokumin Taiiku no Kata. These will give you a grounding in the Judo striking techniques and specific self-defence situations.

Common to all Japanese martial arts are certain principles, and since these apply to self-defence Judo we will look at them briefly.

Heijoshin

This means 'everyday mind'. Compare your state of mind as you walk down to the corner store to buy something, with your state of mind after a minor car accident. After the accident, the adrenalin is pumping round the system, you cannot think straight, and perhaps want to get the hell out of it or explode into a furious rage. In self-defence, the psychological shock is the worst thing to contend with. Thus it is essential to keep your everyday mind, or, more colloquially, keep your cool. This is probably much the same as the mental state of 'hontai' needed in the Koshiki no Kata. To control your mind, control your breathing; and to control your breathing, control your stance. Thus in time of stress, stand straight, square and balanced and take deep, controlled breaths.

Metsuke

One of the problems in combat with another person is where to look. If the eye gets led away by a hand, for example, it may miss a foot that is swinging up. The rule here is not to look at any specific point but just be generally aware of the person in front of you. This is not always as easy as it seems. The opponent may deliberately try to distract you by pointing to something. It takes quite an effort of will not to look. You must be constantly aware of your opponent and not be distracted by anything else. If you feel it necessary to look away, make sure that you step out of range before you do so.

On the other hand, if you want to distract an assailant do it as casually as possible. This is by no means easy but you can practise it in Randori.

Ma-ai

This means 'distance'. The best distance you can have between yourself and an assailant is one where you are beyond his reach but he is within yours.

Between two experienced boxers or Karate fighters, for example, this distance is crucial, but in an ordinary confrontation it is enough to be just out of foot and hand reach. If someone stops you in the street and asks for directions, step casually back, just out of reach, before answering the question.

Shisei

This means 'posture' or 'stance'. In Judo the best fighting stance is the natural stance or 'shizentai'. This has been equated to the Mu no Kamae of Kendo (Japanese sword fighting), and means the Posture of Nothingness. It is the posture that shows nothing to the opponent, giving no intentions away.

Consider what happens when a boxer puts up his hands or a Karate fighter goes into his deep stance. First, it tells you to be ready, and secondly it says something about what sort of attack or defence to expect. The Judo answer is to just stand, relaxed, arms hanging at the side, but acutely aware of what is going on. Looking 'natural' but being very far from that.

The importance of stance in a self-defence situation is that it is the first positive mental and physical move. It shows that you have accepted the possibility of violence and are ready for it. Many people do not really believe that violence can happen to them personally. Consequently when it actually happens they are badly caught out.

Sen

Under the heading of Sen also comes Sensen no Sen and Go no Sen. All three are names for the moments when it is best to make your moves (counter or otherwise) in self-defence.

Sen means attacking a split second after your assailant has started his move. For example, when you see the assailant start to lift his hand (to strike) or step closer (in order to strike), then is the moment to whip in with your own attack.

Sensen no Sen is meant to be the best opportunity of all. It means making your attack between the moment your opponent has made up his mind to strike and the moment he actually starts to strike.

Go no Sen means making your attack after the opponent has made his strike (and missed). For example, he throws in a kick which you see coming and avoid, then instantly you counter-punch, kick or throw.

Zanshin

Zanshin means staying on guard, after you have dealt with your assailant. For example, having avoided a kick or a punch and thrown in your own counter-attack, the assailant may drop to the floor and appear finished. However, he could well be faking or just momentarily stunned. Having made your move, it is important to back off from your opponent still facing him, or, if you have to go closer, do so very carefully and from an angle that would make it difficult for him to strike or catch hold.

When facing an armed assailant the first thing to realise is that you are at a serious disadvantage and that confrontation is best avoided, if at all possible. If you have to defend yourself in this situation, there are two main rules. The first is that whatever move you make, you must move out of the main line of fire. If a man is thrusting at you with a knife, do not stay where you are and tackle him because if you fumble the move the knife will go into you. Combine your defensive move with a step to one side or the other. The other main rule is deal with the weapon before the man. Try to strike the weapon down using whatever weapon you yourself can find, then attack your assailant.

Facing a number of attackers is the same as facing an armed assailant. Avoid the situation if at all possible. Just run away and forget your pride. If you have no choice but to fight, go for the leader of the pack hard and fast; if he goes down the rest may run. Avoid going to the ground at all costs, but if you do get knocked down, curl up tightly, preferably in a corner or against a wall which will give your body some protection and take special care of your head. If possible try to lead the fight to a terrain which will give you the advantage. For example, choose a narrow doorway or alley where your attackers can only come at you one at a time. Get the sun behind you and fight from higher ground such as a stairway. Look for anything that can be used as a weapon.

If looking for a weapon, remember that most objects can be used either to momentarily distract, blind or stun an attacker. If you find a stick or similar long object, do not swing blindly at your attacker. In this case the rule is, go for the bones. For example, it is no good connecting with some fleshy part of the assailant, it will not hurt him enough. Aim for the bony areas such as the wrists, elbows, knees and ankles. A sharp blow delivered here is excruciatingly painful. If your attacker is holding a weapon, then strike at his wrist or elbow.

Preceding any of the above actions should be a long, cool look at the situation you are in or heading for. Accept firstly that violence is possible if the situation has that potential. Do not walk blithely along a dark road or in a dangerous part of town and hope that nothing will happen.

Look at your surroundings. Potential weapons must be spied out, possible help, escape routes if you have to run, narrow alleyways, doorways, higher ground, good footing for yourself and bad footing for your assailant. Anything that may be of use must be looked for.

Self-defence is not just a collection of tricks learned in three easy lessons. Acquiring a good judgement of the situation and keeping cool need practice. One of the best ways to approximate to this is to practise a combat art, such as Judo, boxing, Karate or wrestling; then the essential background to the tricks will be learned.

Remember, finally, that there are legal limits to the amount of force you may use when defending yourself. You are required to avoid violence where possible, no matter how cowardly you may feel that to be, and that when *defence* is unavoidable that the force returned is reasonable and just sufficient for the situation. You must not use a sledge-hammer to crack a nut.

In fact there is a sort of Catch-22 situation with regard to the law and self-defence. If you are unaware of any self-defence techniques and manage to deal with an assailant 'reasonably' it is not likely that you will be prosecuted for any injury done to the assailant. If on the other hand you become expert at one of the martial arts and deal with an attacker, a judge may regard your special knowledge and ability as an offensive weapon and prosecute you for any injury offered to the other party. The average person in the street may well regard this situation as ridiculous and feel that he has a right to learn to defend himself. It is as well to realise that the law sometimes thinks otherwise.

Judo training will give you awareness, fitness and confidence and these three qualities will be more valuable in avoiding violence than any specific techniques for dealing with it.

15

Judo Philosophy, Etiquette and Discipline

Judo philosophy

The very name of Judo indicates that there is meant to be more to it than just fighting techniques. JU, of course, means non-resisting but DO (Chinese TAO as in Taoism) means the Way.

The earliest mention of the word JU-DO is in the chronicles of the Chinese emperor Kuang Wu of the later Han dynasty, who lived in the first half of the first century AD. Here it means not a martial art, but the principle of having a compliant, yielding attitude.

Much later, and especially in Japan, the suffix DO came to be used in the specific sense of being a Way or means to self-realisation, or a deeper understanding of one's own nature and the world in general. Being a vehicle, or a means to understanding, the activity itself is nothing unless it leads to insight. In much the same way a book is nothing more than ink and paper if its contents are not understood.

In 1882, Jigoro Kano abandoned the word Ju-jitsu (techniques of non-resistance) and renamed his art JU-DO, indicating that it was as much educational as physical.

Judo, being oriental, is the way to an understanding of basically oriental concepts, but any complicated activity, Eastern or Western, if deeply looked into, offers truths not immediately apparent.

Why Judo and not football, for example, you may ask; and the answer is that the martial arts are particularly suited for vehicles of understanding in that they are 'sudden-death' activities that test in the most direct and immediate way particular human qualities. A moment's relaxation means defeat.

The context of Judo is 'the fight'; to many people a fundamentally unpleasant situation where two people are directly striving to overcome each other. The outcome is victory and defeat for one or other of the combatants and there are no margins for rest; the fight is here and now and must be resolved. Not only must difficult technique be mastered, but courage, candid self-appraisal and determination are required. The training is hard and often painful and the participant learns the boundaries of his physical and mental capabilities.

From the first, the trainee must learn to reverse certain of his 'natural' reactions. Push a non-Judo person and he will push back, but push a Judoka and he will go with the push and the pusher may find himself flat on the floor. Learning to fall is another 'unnatural' thing for a Judoka to do. The Judoka must learn to live with physical (and mental) insecurity. At any moment in a Judo fight he may be catapulted from a secure, comfortable position into the void. Compare the extreme nervousness of a beginner with that of the expert who can 'let himself go' in any situation. Indeed the stress in Judo is on 'letting go,' physically and mentally. By letting go and relaxing in one of the most frightening of human situations – the fight – he can learn something about himself and that mind or ego which appears to direct him. By constantly fighting people he learns, or should learn, about other people and how they react, and nearly all this knowledge can be used in daily life.

Various Eastern philosophies and religions are associated with Judo and these will be briefly looked at.

Kodokan Judo philosophy

Jigoro Kano constructed his system complete with physical and moral principles. In his writings he rejected religion, which presumably meant such Eastern ones as Buddhism, and embraced morality – indicating a more Confucian approach to life and Judo. He was educated in both the Chinese classical tradition and the modern Western one. In contrast to the other Japanese martial arts, his approach could be said to be more Western or Utilitarian, though of course Chinese classical education includes ideas by such utilitarian philosophers as Mo Tzu.

Kano enshrined his principles in two catch-phrases Seiryoku-zenyo and Jitakyoei. The first means 'good use of mind and body' which has been paraphrased, 'maximum efficiency, minimum effort'. This is said to be a step further than the Chinese concept of JU, or giving way. For example, if pushed, a Judoman will give way and use the push of the opponent; but if the opponent catches hold of the wrist there is no way to 'give way'. The wrist is caught and must be freed. In this case the grip can be broken by working on the weak point of the grip, namely the thumb, and this is an example of using one's strength effectively or efficiently. The Judoman is expected to look for the easy way of doing things.

Jitakyoei is translated as 'mutual welfare and benefit' and means: one best helps oneself by helping others. Helping others becomes very apparent in Judo. Judo is fought within rules, but it would not be difficult to abuse them. In Randori the possibility exists of injuring or even killing the opponent, and self-restraint must be used. Care is taken not to injure the other party and similar care is expected in return. The higher grades must look after the lower grades and similarly the stronger ones must not abuse the weaker ones.

The three traditional objectives or purposes of Judo are Shobuho (combat), Taiikuho (physical training) and Shushinho (ethical training).

The principle of Shobuho is said to be expressed in the following verse:

> In victory be not proud of winning,
> In defeat be not downcast,
> When the going is easy do not be careless,
> When the going is tough do not be afraid,
> Just tread the one [middle] Way.

Shushinho has three subdivisions. The first is the cultivation of virtue, the second is the training of the intellect, and the third is the application of contest principles to everyday affairs. The last is considered especially important. The Judoka is expected to apply what he learns to his everyday affairs outside Judo.

Zen in Judo

Although Zen is often associated with Judo, Kano did not make it part of his philosophy. Nevertheless, other martial arts such as sword-fighting, and Ju-jitsu had long been regarded as suitable vehicles for understanding Zen ideas and Judo was regarded by the Zen experts as being similarly suitable.

One description of Buddhism, of which Zen is a sect, is that it is a pragmatic psychology – a description of the mind (which includes the body and emotions for the Buddhists do not believe that body and mind etc. are separable), and its workings, based upon many centuries of experimentation.

At the top level of any well-developed sport the technical differences between the leading players are so small as to be of little significance and what distinguishes the real champion is his mental approach to his game. In a martial art, having the right mental approach was of, literally, vital significance.

Many Japanese swordsmen turned to Zen for their mental training and it is significant that men such as Miyamoto Musashi who had survived over fifty real sword-fights, wrote Zen classics (see his *Gori nosho – Five Rings* and works by Daisetsu Suzuki).

One of the central ideas of Buddhism and Zen, is that the existence of a Self which we think we have in our everyday life is but an illusion, and that all desires that are attached to this self-illusion are also illusory. The true self is revealed when the unenlightened self evaporates. In Zen this is called the reawakening of the non-ego to its own essence.

On a practical level, the illusions of the Self such as pride, fear, greed and lust are an obstacle to the ultimate mastery of a skill such as Judo or Kendo. The belief that a Self exists which can control events, and that this Self requires such things as fame or money, leads to a sort of freezing of the mind. It ceases to be able to see what simply *is* but sees everything in terms of its goal (fame etc.) and the futile attempt to direct itself towards that goal. Not being able to see what *is*, is of course, dangerous in a fighting situation.

In such a situation the mind must be fluid but the mind has the strong tendency to hang on to whatever it currently values. Attack a man carrying a small package and you will see that his immediate reaction is to hang on to the package rather than adequately defend himself. He may first think where he can put the package down but he will not simply let the package go and bring up his arms to protect himself.

In Judo, a position is held for as long as it is necessary, but when it becomes unnecessary it is let go, with not a moment's thought. Letting go is one of the important Judo techniques, and when this can be transferred to such grasped after things as fame and fortune, from a

Zen point of view the Judoka can be truly said to be an expert.

The mind, believing that it can control events, enters a Judo contest thinking, 'if he does this, I will do that', or, 'I will throw him with such and such a throw' but this freezes the mind and delays total and adequate response to the real situation. Such is the swift flow of attack and defence in Judo that just pausing to think leaves you open to attack.

At first Judo techniques have to be consciously mastered but at some point the Judoka must learn to let go and trust his training. Letting go when fighting is at first real brinkmanship, but once it is discovered that the body fights better when the thinking mind is not trying to direct every move, confidence grows and spontaneous techniques occur.

Spontaneity, and total commitment and experience are some of the features of Zen Judo. 'Entering at a stroke' is one of the Zen principles; in a Judo context this means to be able to hurl oneself into an attack, regardless of the consequences for oneself, as soon as an opening is intuited. 'Holding tightly – letting go lightly' is another Zen flavoured catch-phrase. When a tight hold is required, it should be tight, but the moment it is no longer needed, the hold evaporates like a snowflake settling on a fire. In Judo the breaks are clean and the fight flows on.

Part of the total experience of Judo are the Summer and Winter Special Training Periods (Shochugeiko and Kangeiko). Here the Judoka undergoes training for one month during the hottest and coldest times of the year. By undergoing this severe training, the boundaries of the illusory Self are explored and transcended, and in this way the trainee begins to understand the expression, 'knowing warmth and coolness towards oneself'.

Ultimately, both Judo and Zen put their emphasis on freedom and creativity. From its earliest days the human mind is trained to see things in terms of laws, symbols, similarities, opposites, values, which are not things in themselves but a sort of grid put over reality in an attempt to understand it better. The word 'bottle', for example, is merely a sound or a string of six letters. It is never quite the same as the thing that cuts you when it breaks, or from which you drink wine. In Zen the object is to experience the reality and not the symbol. When this is experienced, true freedom (freedom from the tyranny of the mind) is gained and in this freedom creativity occurs.

Similarly, in Judo, the beginner is first shown 'correct' technique, and rigid Kata. He is taught 'patterns' of movement selected out of the vast complexity of Judo movements. At first the Judoka must subdue his ego somewhat and learn the techniques as taught. However, when these have been mastered, he is expected to go beyond this formal teaching and discover the reality of Judo for himself.

By letting go mentally and physically, and experiencing 'no-hindrance', his awareness becomes full and every action is experienced as a vital freedom. Ultimately, the Judoka is to be not just as good as his teacher but to 'stand on his shoulders'.

In a Zen Buddhist monastery, the central technique for seeing what *is* and achieving the awakening of the non-ego to its own essence, is sitting meditation, or Zazen. For years the trainees meditate many hours a day, in addition to the daily monastic routine. In Judo, the awakening is achieved by *total* immersion in Judo and a small amount of meditation. It is common in most Dojos in Japan to finish a training session with a few minutes of Mokuso, or sitting meditation, although by monastic standards this is merely a drop in the ocean.

Taoism in Judo

In Taoism and in Judo the stress is on 'wu-wei' or 'not doing' or 'letting happen'. In Judo you have to live on the very frontiers of the action, not a thought away from it, and when you can learn to 'not-do', the most unexpected can occur. Of course, this presupposes that technique has been learnt. Once a throw has been learnt well and the mental block is removed, throws occur 'out of the blue' and very spectacularly. However, maintaining this attitude in a fight is highly difficult. The Taoist expression goes

'The stillness in stillness is not the real stillness; only where there is stillness in movement does the Universal rhythm manifest itself'.

Although these various facets of Judo are said to exist, the point must be made that one does not naturally acquire these virtues or insights by simply doing Judo even to a very intensive level. Napoleon's donkey is said to have accompanied him on all his campaigns but obviously learnt nothing. The psychological problems may well not become apparent. What is needed is a keen mind or a teacher perceptive enough to point them out.

When Judo is done as a means to understand these philosophies it is done as a 'Shugyo', that is to say as an ascetic practice. This means doing it to the exclusion of all else, enduring pain and exhaustion, setbacks and triumphs. Judo is still largely regarded as a Shugyo in Japan and is practised as such.

Etiquette and discipline

The rules for Kodokan Judo trainees were first formulated in 1894, revised in 1912 and are still in force, unchanged, today. They are:

1. Those who do Judo must pledge to benefit the state and mankind through the training of their bodies.
2. On entering and leaving the Dojo a bow is to be made in the direction of the Master's seat.
3. When in the Dojo the directions of the teachers, officials and senior grades are to be obeyed.
4. Etiquette is to be maintined towards the teachers, senior grades and officials. Advanced Judoka must look after and lead the less advanced, and they in turn must follow this lead.
5. On entering the Dojo, Judoka must sign the Register.
6. Unreasonable absence is not permitted, unless on account of illness or other unavoidable reasons. However, those requesting a practice must gain permission in advance.
7. Change of guarantor or address is to be notified.
8. Dress should be Hakama or Western dress.
9. No nakedness is allowed outside the changing rooms. No smoking.
10. When in the Dojo sit or stand correctly. Never sit with knees sticking up, lie down, have hands in pockets, or have legs sticking out.
11. Those living in Tokyo should present to their teacher and colleagues one piece of Kagami-mochi (rice cake) as a New Year gift.
12. Those living afar or those ill should send New Year greetings by post and inform of new address.
13. All Judoka should participate in the Spring and Autumn Red and White contests and the Monthly promotional contests. If unable to participate, the contests must be watched.
14. Conform to the true spirit of Judo, always foster a sincere heart, respect morality, discharge your duties, be prudent in your conduct, be hygienic, and, with regard to all things, be of right mind.

Of these fourteen articles, numbers one and fourteen are deemed to be the most important. Obviously some of these articles apply to the Japanese only and those living in Tokyo; however, most of them are still applicable in the West.

As can be seen in article No. 2, it is customary to make a (standing) bow when entering and leaving the Dojo. This is usually done at the entrance to where the actual training takes place. All Dojos in Japan and many outside follow this tradition. The Master's seat or dais is usually opposite the entrance, with perhaps a separate entrance for instructors.

At the start of a session it is customary for all to line up in the Japanese kneeling manner (sitting on the heels) with the students drawn up in order of rank facing the Master's dais (Joza or Kamiza) and with the teachers facing them, also in order of rank, backs to the dais. The senior student makes the command – Sensei ni Rei! (bow to the teachers!) and all make a kneeling bow to each other. The teachers may then bow to each other. This ceremony is also done at the finish of a training session.

During the session, at the start and finish of each Randori bout, the practitioners make a standing or kneeling bow to each other – the teacher or senior of the two having the Dais on his right. Teachers generally merit a kneeling bow, and the Randori bow should usually be done at the edge of the mat.

The atmosphere in a Dojo should be quiet, hardworking and simple. When there are a lot of experienced people working together this is usually so, but when younger people are training this mood can degenerate into horseplay. Judo is potentially a dangerous activity and it is essential to maintain discipline in the Dojo to prevent injuries.

Japanese discipline and etiquette may seem irrelevant to Westerners but it is all part of the 'style' or image of Judo. Remove the Japanese aspects, and if you are strictly logical this would mean doing away with judogi, belts, bare feet and terminology, and you are left with an undistinguished form of wrestling which would probably appeal to nobody.

Appendix - Contest Rules

Summary of contest rules   (International Judo Federation)

1. The competition area shall be a maximum of 16 m (17 yd) × 16 m (17 yd) and a minimum of 14 m (15 yd) × 14 m (15 yd).
2. The contestants shall wear a Judogi (judo costume)
    (a) the sleeves shall be loose and long enough to cover more than half the forearm.
    (b) the trousers shall be loose and long enough to cover more than half the lower leg.
3. The contestants shall keep their nails cut short and not wear any metallic article which may possibly injure or endanger the opponent.
4. The contest shall start with both contestants facing each other approximately 4 m (4 yd) apart in a standing position. After making a standing bow the contest will begin after the referee's command of Hajime (begin!).
5. The contest ends with the referee's call of Sore Made! (finish).
6. The contest shall be judged on the basis of throwing techniques and ground techniques (throws, pins, arm-locks and strangles).
7. The contest shall end there and then if one contestant scores Ippon (full winning score – 10 points).
8. Groundwork may occur in the following cases:
    (a) Following a partially completed throw.
    (b) when either party falls to the ground following an unsuccessfully completed throw.

(c) continuing a lock or strangle on the ground after it has taken effect in the standing position.

(d) when the opponent is swiftly tumbled to the ground with a movement other than a recognised throw.

(e) when one party goes to the ground for any reason not covered by the preceding, the other party may attack with groundwork.

9. The duration of a contest shall not be less than three minutes or more than twenty minutes.

10. Any technique that coincided with the signal for the end of the contest shall be recognised as valid. A hold-down called just before time will be allowed to run its full thirty seconds and be recognised as valid.

11. Hold-downs will be invalidated once both parties completely leave the area.

12. The majority decision of the two judges and the referee is final and without appeal.

13. An Ippon scores 10 points, a Waza-ari scores 7 points, a Yuko scores 5 points and a Koka scores 3 points. These scores will be announced by the referee as he assesses the technique made.

14. Two scores of Waza-ari combine to win the contest there and then. Scores below Waza-ari do not accumulate.

15. When the referee considers a hold-down has been successfully applied he will announce 'Osaekomi!'. Should the hold-down be broken before the thirty seconds has elapsed he will call 'Toketa!'.

16. If no score has been made by the end of the contest, the referee will announce 'Hantei!' (Decision!) and the two judges will indicate with their flags who they think the winner is.

17. The referee shall add his own opinion to that of the judges and award the decision (victory) on a majority basis.

18. The contest may be temporarily stopped by the referee on his announcement of Matte! (stop) and shall recommence with his announcement of Hajime! (begin). Similarly, the announcement Sono-mama (as you are) freezes the contestants and Yoshi! (carry on) unfreezes them.

19. *Prohibited acts*

The following acts are prohibited:

(a) Sweeping away the thrower's supporting leg from the inside so as to throw him on his front when he has moved into position for his throw (e.g. Harai-goshi) (*b*) to throw by entwining legs (grapevining)

(*c*) squeezing the opponent's trunk, neck or head with the legs

(*d*) to make joint-locks on any other joint than the elbow joint

(*e*) make any action that may injure the neck or spinal column of the opponent

(*f*) lifting a supine opponent off the mat in order to drive him back into the mat

(*g*) intentionally falling backwards when the opponent is clinging to the back

(*h*) breaking the opponent's grip on the jacket by kicking it

(*i*) avoiding contact with the opponent and avoiding the contest

(*j*) intentionally going outside the contest area or forcing the opponent out

(*k*) adopting an excessively defensive posture in order to avoid defeat

(*l*) continually holding the opponent's collar, lapel or sleeve on the same side with both hands, or the opponent's belt or bottom of his jacket with either or both hands.

(*m*) inserting one or more fingers into the opponent's sleeve or trouser bottom or grasping by screwing up the sleeve

(*n*) standing continually with the fingers of one or both hands interlocked with those of the opponent in order to prevent action in the contest

(*o*) intentionally disarranging one's Judogi or belt without the referee's permission

(*p*) pulling the opponent down in order to start groundwork

(*q*) going to groundwork by grabbing foot or leg, unless the movement is done skilfully

(*r*) binding any part of the opponent's body with the belt or jacket

(*s*) taking the opponent's jacket in the mouth or placing hand, arm, foot or leg on the opponent's face

(*t*) placing the foot or leg inside the jacket or trousers and bending the opponent's fingers in order to break his grip

(*u*) failing to let go when the opponent has lifted you clear of the mat or is in a position to lift

(*v*) applying any technique outside the contest area

(*w*) disregarding the referee's instructions

(*x*) making unnecessary calls, remarks or gestures derogatory to the opponent (*y*) making any other action which may injure or endanger the opponent or may be against the spirit of Judo. Any contestant who performs or attempts to perform any of the above acts shall be liable for disqualification or other disciplinary action by the referee in accordance with the Rules.

20. The following penalty scores are given according to the severity of the infringement: Shido (3-points), Chui (5-points), Keikoku (7-points) and Hansokumake (10-points). Simple repetition of any penalty will merit a penalty score of the next level.

21. An Ippon is awarded in the following cases:

(*a*) when the contestant applying the technique, or countering or avoiding his opponent's technique, throws him largely on his back with considerable force or impetus

(*b*) when one contestant skilfully lifts his opponent who is lying with his back on the mat, up to about the height of his own shoulders

(*c*) when one contestant says 'Maitta' (I give in) or taps his or his opponent's body or the mat with his hand or foot two or more times

(*d*) when one contestant holds the other, unable to get away for thirty seconds after the announcement of Osaekomi (holding)

(*e*) when the effect of a strangle or joint-lock is sufficiently apparent

22. A Waza-ari (7-points) is assessed as follows:

(*a*) when a throw is not quite successful in terms of landing on back and impetus

(*b*) when a hold-down is held from twenty-five to twenty-nine seconds

23. A Yuko (5-points) and Koka (3-points) when given for throws are assessed in terms of degree of impetus and on what part of the body the opponent lands, in relation to an Ippon throw. A hold-down held for twenty to twenty-four seconds scores 5 points (Yuko), and held for ten to nineteen seconds scores Koka (3 points).

Glossary

Ashi	Foot, leg
Ashi-barai	Foot sweep
Ashi-waza	Foot techniques
Atemi	Striking techniques
Chui	5-point penalty
Dan	Advanced grades
-do	A Way, Art
Dojo	Training hall
Futanren	Insufficient training
Gasshuku	Training camp
Go	Hard, resistant
Gokyo	The five teachings (forty throws)
Goshinjitsu	Self-defence techniques
Gyaku	Joint-locks
Hadaka-jime	Naked choke
Hane-goshi	Spring hip-throw
Hansokumake	Disqualification
Hantei!	Decision!

Harai-goshi	Sweeping hip-throw
Heijoshin	Everyday mind
Hikiwake	Drawn competition
Hineri-jime	Twisting strangle
Hiza-guruma	Knee wheel-throw
Hontai	Immoveable mind
Ippon	Winning technique (10 points)
Ippon Seoi-nage	One-arm shoulder-throw
Itsutsu no Kata	The Kata of five movements
Jigotai	Defensive stance
Jitakyoei	Mutual welfare and benefit
Ju	Compliant, yielding
Judo	Martial Art founded by Jigoro Kano
Judogi	Judo costume
Judoka	Judo practitioner
Juji-gatame	Cross arm-lock
Juji-jime	Cross strangle
Ju-jitsu	Unarmed combat systems
Ju no Kata	The Kata of Ju (of non-resistance)
Kaeshi-waza	Counter-throws
Kamishiho-gatame	Upper four quarters hold-down
Kangeiko	Mid-Winter Special Training
Kansetsu-waza	Joint-locks
Kata	Pre-arranged sequences
Kata-gatame	Shoulder hold-down
Kata-guruma	Shoulder wheel-throw
Kata-hajime	Single wing strangle
Katame no Kata	The Kata of groundwork
Katame-waza	Groundwork techniques
Keikoku	7-point penalty
Kesa-gatame	Scarf hold-down
Kiki-oji	Hear and tremble
Kime no Kata	The Kata of decisive techniques
Kodokan	Original Judo HQ
Kogi	Lectures
Kohaku-shiai	Red and White Contests

Koka	3-point score
Koshi/goshi	Hip
Koshi-guruma	Hip wheel-throw
Koshiki no Kata	The Kata of ancient forms
Kosoto-gari	Minor outer reaping-throw
Ko-uchi-gari	Minor inner reaping-throw
Kuzushi	Balance breaking
Kyu	Beginner grade
Kyusho	Vital nerve spot
Ma-ai	Fighting distance
Maitta!	I give in/submit!
Metsuke	Focus
Mikuzure	See and crumble
Mokuso	Meditation
Mondo	Question and answer
Morote Seoi-nage	Double-arm shoulder-throw
Nage no Kata	The Kata of throws
Nage-waza	Throwing techniques
Ne-waza	Groundwork
O-goshi	Major hip-throw
O-guruma	Major wheel-throw
Okuri-ashi-harai	Double foot sweep-throw
Okuri-eri-jime	Sliding collar strangle
Osaekomi!	Holding!
Osaekomi-waza	Hold-downs
Osoto-gari	Major outer reaping-throw
O-uchi-gari	Major inner reaping-throw
Randori	Free-fighting
Rei	Bow
Renraku-waza	Combination techniques
Sankaku-jime	Triangular strangle
Seoi-otoshi	Shoulder drop-throw
Seiryoku-Zenyo	Best use of mind and body

Seiryoku-Zenyo Kokumin Taiiku no Kata	The Kata of the people's physical education in the (principle of) best use of mind and body
Sensei	Teacher, senior
Shiai	Contest
Shido	Caution
Shime-waza	Strangles/chokes
Shisei	Posture
Shizentai	Natural posture
Shobu(ho)	Competition, combat
Shochugeiko	Mid-summer Special Training
Shugyo	Ascetic training
Shushin(ho)	Ethical/moral training
Sono-mama!	Stay as you are/freeze!
Sore-made!	Finish!
Sukashi	Side-step
Sutemi-waza	Sacrifice throws
Tachi-waza	Standing techniques/throws
Tai-iku(ho)	Physical training
Tai-otoshi	Body-drop throw
Tao	The Way (Chinese)
Tateshiho-gatame	Lengthwise four quarters hold-down
Te-guruma	Hand wheel (counter-throw)
Te-waza	Hand arm-throw
Toketa!	Hold-down broken!
Tokui-waza	Favourite technique
Tomoe-nage	Stomach throw
Tsuri-komi-ashi	Propping drawing ankle-throw
Tsuri-komi-goshi	Propping drawing hip-throw
Tsuri-goshi	Drawing hip-throw
Uchi-komi	Repetition training, drills
Uchi-mata	Inner thigh-throw
Ude-garami	Entangled arm-lock
Ude-gatame	Arm-press lock
Ukemi	Breakfalls
Uki-waza	Floating throw
Ushiro-kesa-gatame	Rear scarf hold-down

Waki-gatame	Arm-pit lock
-waza	Technique
Waza-ari	7-point score
Wu-wei	Not-doing (Chinese)
Yoko-gake	Side dash throw
Yokoshiho-gatame	Side four quarters hold-down
Yoshi!	Carry on!
Yuko	5-point score
Zanshin	Attentiveness
Zazen	Sitting in meditation
Zen	Meditative state, Buddhist school

Pronunciation

All the vowels are sounded. 'Sore made' is pronounced 'sorry mahday.' 'Ei' is pronounced 'ay' in 'day', 'Ai' is pronounced 'y' as in 'my', 'Ae' is pronounced 'ah-eh.' Syllables are evenly stressed.

Index

KARATE

ERIC DOMINY

Karate is the most effective form of self-defence, and one of the toughest forms of physical training possible. Anyone, of any age, can practise it, and practise alone. No special equipment is required and, with reasonable precautions, there is no danger.

   This fully illustrated book by one of the founders of the London Karate Kai is designed as an introduction to Karate for the beginner. Each major school has developed its own system of Karate, so Eric Dominy covers a series of basic movements, arising from some of the Basic Postures. This forms a perfect foundation for further instruction at an approved club.

TEACH YOURSELF BOOKS

RUNNING TO KEEP FIT

BRIAN MITCHELL

What are the physiological rewards of running? What biochemical changes occur when exercising? How are the heart and blood vessels affected?

Brian Mitchell shows that running to keep fit is one of the simplest, cheapest, most practical and enjoyable means of attaining physical fitness. He explains the principles of training, what to do, where, how and when to run, how to measure progress and overcome difficulties. He has had many years' experience of coaching club and senior athletics and uses his knowledge of specialist running to help the beginner.

Brian Mitchell is also the author of *Running To Win* in the Teach Yourself series.

TEACH YOURSELF BOOKS